The Evolution
of Mozart's
Pianistic
Style

*

Mario R. Mercado, m. R.

Southern
Illinois
University
Carbondale　　Press　　*Edwardsville*

Copyright © 1992 by the Board of Trustees, Southern Illinois University

Printed in the United States of America

Designed by David Ford

Production supervised by Natalia Nadraga

95 94 93 92   4   3   2   1

Frontispiece: Close-up of the keyboard of Mozart's pianoforte made by Anton Walter (c. 1780), photograph courtesy of the Internationale Stiftung Mozarteum Salzburg, photograph copyright O. Anrather, Salzburg, Austria.

Library of Congress Cataloging-in-Publication Data
Mercado, Mario Raymond, 1956–
    The evolution of Mozart's pianistic style / Mario R. Mercado.
    p.   cm.
Includes bibliographical references and index.
    1. Mozart, Wolfgang Amadeus, 1756–1791. Piano Music. 2.
Piano music—18th century—History and criticism. I. Title.
ML410.M9M45   1992
786.2'092—dc20   91-8698
ISBN 0-8093-1690-0   CIP
                                           MN

The paper used in this publication meets the minimum requirements of American National Standard for Information Sciences—Permanence of Paper for Printed Library Materials, ANSI Z39.48-1984. ∞

2/92 3/07

For my parents

Contents

✳

Contents

Preface

*

In the immense picture of Mozart's work, a special perspective arises through the evolution of his keyboard music. As the documents of his life attest, Mozart was an eminent performer on the organ, harpsichord, and clavichord, but it was the piano that became his favorite, his "personal" instrument in settings ranging from the classical orchestral texture of the piano concerto to the most intimate solo literature seemingly addressed to no other audience than the composer himself. Mozart's short life coincided with the rise of the piano, and a shift in musical taste produced new ideals of instrumental sound as well as new instrumental genres specifically linked to these ideals. The development of keyboard practice in the eighteenth century is complex and marked by subtly varying trends, and in Mozart's work, many of these trends characteristically merge. Certain pieces reflect keyboard traditions rooted in the late Baroque. Others, particularly the sonatas, outline the road through a midcentury style to Viennese Classicism, while isolated ones from his last years point to a style beyond his time.

*

In the vast and ever-growing literature devoted to Mozart, one book, published in 1955 in anticipation of the two-hundredth anniversary of the composer's birth, was to assume a special place, Hanns Dennerlein's *Der unbekannte Mozart: Die Welt seiner Klavierwerke*. It was the first monograph dealing with Mozart's entire keyboard oeuvre. Set within a chronological frame, it provided a stylistic overview of Mozart's music from the perspective of keyboard composition.

The title of Dennerlein's work presented two specific challenges. It reminded the reader that the world of Mozart's keyboard music had remained to some extent that of the *unbekannte Mozart* (the unknown Mozart). Dennerlein's principal aim was to move to the forefront a segment of Mozart's work that must be considered on a par with the composer's achievements in the genres of opera, symphony, and string quartet.

Yet this aim involved a second, more intricate challenge that, to the English-speaking reader, is somewhat obscured by the German terminology: in his choice of title, Dennerlein was compelled to speak of Mozart's keyboard works as his *Klavierwerke.* The complexity of this term invites further study tracing the course of terminological usage from the general designation *keyboard* to the special designation *piano,* which the German language has never fully recognized and for which the overall design of Dennerlein's presentation provided no room.

✳

Consideration of the eighteenth-century changes in keyboard mechanism is meaningful only in the context of stylistic evolution as linked to the exigencies, advantages, and impetus of the medium. The special quality of the eighteenth-century piano, and Mozart's piano in particular, must be examined. Nevertheless, such an investigation cannot be limited to purely technical dictates, though these may have inspired stylistic innovation. Rather, it is the innately artistic innovation, resulting in the creation of a totally new literature and influencing the whole creative career of the composer, which is bound to become the central issue for a discussion of the origin and growth of Mozart's specifically pianistic style and which is the subject of this book.

The development of such a style is paralleled to some extent in the works of such composers as Carl Philipp Emanuel Bach, Johann Christian Bach, Haydn, and Clementi. Yet the activities of the former two end, and a discernible pianistic idiom in the works of the latter merely begins at the time of crucial changes in Mozart's keyboard writing. Haydn's keyboard oeuvre, unlike Clementi's, obviously comparable to Mozart's in so many ways, is not of a comparable scope; his commitment to the keyboard genre never moves out of the shadow of his commitment to the quartet or the symphony.

In his unique contribution to the evolution of keyboard literature, Mozart might be considered the heir of Johann Sebastian Bach. As Bach virtually created the keyboard concerto, so Mozart virtually created new keyboard genres. The rising span of keyboard styles, prophetically summarized in the two ricercari from Bach's *Musical Offering,*[1] dominated Mozart's keyboard writing and decisively contributed to its most mature phase. Haydn did not have a "Bach-Erlebnis" similar to Mozart's,[2] and while the impact of Haydn's classical polyphony was to guide Mozart in the composition of string quartets, it was the polyphony of the Baroque that was to guide Mozart's keyboard works to culmination. Within the development leading from harpsichord to piano, Mozart's achievement stands alone in its time and in history, and the evolution of the pianistic style must always be seen as linked in a very special way to Mozart.

Acknowledgments

✳

My greatest debt of gratitude is to Alfred Mann whose critical insight and inestimable guidance have been the good omens of this study. Robert Phillips, acquisitions editor, Southern Illinois University Press, provided editorial help with great care and sensitivity. I appreciate his experience, his kind and patient support, and his enthusiastic interest in the topic.

I wish to thank Eva Badura-Skoda for reading an early draft and offering valuable comments. My investigations benefited immeasurably from many suggestions received from Malcolm Bilson who gave freely of his admirable expertise, calling my attention to aspects of Mozart's writing with regard to contemporary instruments and performance practices.

A number of individuals contributed information, materials, and assistance that facilitated my work: Rudolf Angermüller, Generalsekretär, Internationale Stiftung Mozarteum; Robert Bailey, professor of musicology, New York University; Nancy Calocerinos, Rochester, New York; Amy Daken, New York City; Jane Gottlieb, head librarian, The Juilliard School; Dieter Heuler, Koch International, Düsseldorf; Erna Schwerin, president, Friends of Mozart, New York; John Shepard, head, rare books and manuscripts, music division, New York Public Library; Joan Swanekamp, head of technical services, Sibley Music Library, Eastman School of Music; and J. Rigbie Turner, curator of music manuscripts, Pierpont Morgan Library. To all of them go my sincere thanks.

Ross Wood, music librarian, Wellesley College, untiringly answered numerous and detailed research and bibliographical questions, and I am grateful for his friendship and kind help. Mention must be made of Sandra P. Rosenblum's gracious response to my questions about eighteenth-century pianos and of Gerald Warfield's valued advice concerning questions of design and printing. For the permission to reproduce music examples from the *Neue Mozart-Ausgabe*, acknowledgment is made to the Bärenreiter-Verlag and its American representative, Foreign Music Distributors.

Finally, special words of appreciation go to my colleagues at the Kurt Weill Foundation for Music for encouragement and support throughout the preparation of this study. David Farneth, the Foundation's director and archivist, generously offered advice ranging from music sources to computer applications, and John Watson provided gratefully received help in a variety of tasks.

Credits

✳

3.1. Concerto in D Major K. 175, 1st movement.
NMA, V/15/1, mm. 67–71.
© Copyright 1972 by Bärenreiter-Verlag; reprinted by permission.

3.2. Concerto in D Major K. 175, 2d movement.
NMA, V/15/1, mm. 23–29.
© Copyright 1972 by Bärenreiter-Verlag; reprinted by permission.

3.3. Variations on a Minuet of J. C. Fischer K. 179 (189a), variation 11.
NMA, IX/26, mm. 42–50.
© Copyright 1961 by Bärenreiter-Verlag; reprinted by permission.

3.4. Variations on a Minuet of J. C. Fischer K. 179 (189a), variation 9.
NMA, IX/26, mm. 1–8.
© Copyright 1961 by Bärenreiter-Verlag; reprinted by permission.

3.5. Sonata in F Major K. 280 (189e), 3d movement.
NMA, IX/25/1, mm. 142–48.
© Copyright 1986 by Bärenreiter-Verlag; reprinted by permission.

3.6. Sonata in D Major K. 284 (205b), 3d movement.
NMA, IX/25/1, mm. 9–17.
© Copyright 1986 by Bärenreiter-Verlag; reprinted by permission.

3.7. Sonata in B-flat Major K. 281 (189f), 3d movement.
NMA, IX/25/1, mm. 52–59.
© Copyright 1986 by Bärenreiter-Verlag; reprinted by permission.

3.8. Sonata in D Major K. 284 (205b), 1st movement.
NMA, IX/25/1, mm. 14–16.
© Copyright 1986 by Bärenreiter-Verlag; reprinted by permission.

3.9. Sonata in D Major K. 284 (205b), 2d movement.
NMA, IX/25/1, mm. 27–36.
© Copyright 1986 by Bärenreiter-Verlag; reprinted by permission.

3.10. Sonata in C Major K. 309 (284b), 1st movement.
NMA, IX/25/1, mm. 8–14.
© Copyright 1986 by Bärenreiter-Verlag; reprinted by permission.

3.11. Sonata in A Minor K. 310 (300d), 1st movement.
NMA, IX/25/1, mm. 1–7.
© Copyright 1986 by Bärenreiter-Verlag; reprinted by permission.

3.12. Sonata in A Minor K. 310 (300d), 2d movement.
NMA, IX/25/1, mm. 81–86.
© Copyright 1986 by Bärenreiter-Verlag; reprinted by permission.

3.13. Sonata in E-flat Major K. 302 (293b) for piano and violin, 2d movement.
NMA, VIII/23/1, mm. 112–17.
© Copyright 1964 by Bärenreiter-Verlag; reprinted by permission.

3.14. Sonata in E Minor K. 304 (300c) for piano and violin, 2d movement.
NMA, VIII/23/1, mm. 94–103.
© Copyright 1964 by Bärenreiter-Verlag; reprinted by permission.

3.15. Sonata in C Major K. 330 (300h), 2d movement.
NMA, IX/25/2, mm. 21–24.
© Copyright 1986 by Bärenreiter-Verlag; reprinted by permission.

3.16. Sonata in F Major K. 332 (300k), 1st movement.
NMA, IX/25/2, mm. 60–67.
© Copyright 1986 by Bärenreiter-Verlag; reprinted by permission.

3.17. Sonata in A Major K. 305 (293d) for piano and violin, 2d movement, variation 3.
NMA, VIII/23/1, mm. 9–14.
© Copyright 1964 by Bärenreiter-Verlag; reprinted by permission.

3.18. Prelude in C Major K. 284a, also known as Capriccio in C Major K. 395 (300g).
NMA, IX/27/2, mm. 7a–7e.
© Copyright 1982 by Bärenreiter-Verlag; reprinted by permission.

3.19. Prelude in C Major K. 284a, also known as Capriccio in C Major K. 395 (300g).
NMA, IX/27/2, mm. 20–25.
© Copyright 1982 by Bärenreiter-Verlag; reprinted by permission.

3.20. Concerto in E-flat Major K. 271, cadenza to 2d movement.
NMA, V/15/2, mm. 5–10.
© Copyright 1976 by Bärenreiter-Verlag; reprinted by permission.

3.21. Concerto in E-flat Major K. 271, alternate cadenza to 1st movement.
NMA, V/15/2, mm. 11–13.
© Copyright 1976 by Bärenreiter-Verlag; reprinted by permission.

3.22. Concerto in E-flat Major K. 271, 1st movement.
NMA, V/15/2, mm. 1–7.
© Copyright 1976 by Bärenreiter-Verlag; reprinted by permission.

4.1. Suite in C Major K. 399 (385i), Sarabande.
NMA, IX/27/2, mm. 1–4.
© Copyright 1982 by Bärenreiter-Verlag; reprinted by permission.

4.2. Fugue in C Minor K. 426 for two pianos.
NMA, IX/24/1, mm. 1–5.
© Copyright 1955 by Bärenreiter-Verlag; reprinted by permission.

4.3. Sonata in E-flat Major K. 380 (374f) for piano and violin, 2d movement.
NMA, VIII/23/2, mm. 15–19.
© Copyright 1965 by Bärenreiter-Verlag; reprinted by permission.

4.4. Sonata in B-flat Major K. 454 for piano and violin, 1st movement.
NMA, VIII/23/2, mm. 5–9.
© Copyright 1965 by Bärenreiter-Verlag; reprinted by permission.

4.5. Sonata in B-flat Major K. 454 for piano and violin, 1st movement.
NMA, VIII/23/2, mm. 98–105.
© Copyright 1965 by Bärenreiter-Verlag; reprinted by permission.

4.6. Quintet in E-flat Major K. 452 for piano and winds, 1st movement.
NMA, VIII/22/1, mm. 56–60.
© Copyright 1957 by Bärenreiter-Verlag; reprinted by permission.

4.7. Quintet in E-flat Major K. 452 for piano and winds, 1st movement.
NMA, VIII/22/1, mm. 44–49.
© Copyright 1957 by Bärenreiter-Verlag; reprinted by permission.

4.8. Concerto in G Major K. 453, 3d movement.
NMA, V/15/5, mm. 104–12.
© Copyright 1965 by Bärenreiter-Verlag; reprinted by permission.

4.9. Concerto in D Minor K. 466, 1st movement.
NMA, V/15/6, mm. 227–30.
© Copyright 1961 by Bärenreiter-Verlag; reprinted by permission.

4.10. Concerto in D Minor K. 466, 2d movement.
NMA, V/15/6, mm. 1–4.
© Copyright 1961 by Bärenreiter-Verlag; reprinted by permission.

4.11. Concerto in E-flat Major K. 482, 3d movement.
NMA, V/15/6, mm. 160–70.
© Copyright 1961 by Bärenreiter-Verlag; reprinted by permission.

4.12. Concerto in C Minor K. 491, 1st movement.
NMA, V/15/7, mm. 283–99.
© Copyright 1959 by Bärenreiter-Verlag; reprinted by permission.

4.13. Concerto in C Major K. 503, 1st movement.
NMA, V/15/7, mm. 276–79.
© Copyright 1959 by Bärenreiter-Verlag; reprinted by permission.

4.14. Fantasy in C Minor K. 475.
NMA, IX/25/2, mm. 125–26.
© Copyright 1986 by Bärenreiter-Verlag; reprinted by permission.

4.15. Sonata in F Major K. 533, 3d movement.
NMA, IX/25/2, mm. 152–60.
© Copyright 1986 by Bärenreiter-Verlag; reprinted by permission.

5.1. Concerto in D Major K. 537, 2d movement.
NMA, V/15/8, mm. 1–4.
© Copyright 1960 by Bärenreiter-Verlag; reprinted by permission.

5.2. Rondo in A Minor K. 511.
NMA, IX/27/2, mm. 1–12.
© Copyright 1982 by Bärenreiter-Verlag; reprinted by permission.

5.3. Rondo in A Minor K. 511.
NMA, IX/27/2, mm. 58–61.
© Copyright 1982 by Bärenreiter-Verlag; reprinted by permission.

5.4. Rondo in A Minor K. 511.
NMA, IX/27/2, mm. 176–82.
© Copyright 1982 by Bärenreiter-Verlag; reprinted by permission.

5.5. Adagio in B Minor K. 540.
NMA, IX/27/2, mm. 1–6.
© Copyright 1982 by Bärenreiter-Verlag; reprinted by permission.

5.6. Adagio in B Minor K. 540.
NMA, IX/27/2, mm. 48–49.
© Copyright 1982 by Bärenreiter-Verlag; reprinted by permission.

5.7. Gigue in G Major K. 574.
NMA, IX/27/2, mm. 1–12; 24–38.
© Copyright 1982 by Bärenreiter-Verlag; reprinted by permission.

5.8. Minuet in D Major K. 355 (594; KV6: 576b).
NMA, IX/27/2, mm. 17–40.
© Copyright 1982 by Bärenreiter-Verlag; reprinted by permission.

The Evolution of Mozart's Pianistic Style

I

The Young Keyboard Virtuoso

> Even the inventor prided himself rather on having revolu-
> tionized the older instruments than on having originated a
> totally distinct one, while the average composer . . . con-
> tinued for some time to write harpsichord music for the
> piano, quite oblivious of the fact that the latter was so en-
> tirely novel a medium as to demand an equally novel style.
> Even a great genius like Mozart, who as a child had been
> trained at the harpsichord, did not adapt himself very suc-
> cessfully to a pianistic manner. His keyboard sonatas and
> concertos were delicious and occasionally sublime music,
> but they are not essentially congenial to the piano in the
> sense that his quartets are adapted to strings or his operatic
> arias to the voice. The truth is, of course, that Mozart
> came into the world before the harpsichord was extinct
> and the piano fully developed, and that he could therefore
> hardly be expected to be quite off with the old love or
> wholeheartedly on with the new.[1]

This judgment is surprising, doubly so since it was written by a Mozart biographer. Mozart's keyboard works played a singular role in his development
as a composer; at the same time this oeuvre, crystallizing a new keyboard
technique, formed the basis of the first genuine body of piano literature. There
can be no denying that Mozart's early compositions are harpsichord pieces,
and yet the evolution from these works to compositions in which the piano
figured decisively in the composer's imagination seems extremely swift. This
is due not only to the brevity of Mozart's life and the intensity of his creative
development but also to the composer's artistic need to find a "voice" that at
once provided him with an intimate means of expression and with the possibility of giving utterance to a novel and personal instrumental idiom.

While there is some truth in the statement that the sonatas and the concertos
"are not essentially congenial to the piano in the sense that his quartets are
adapted to strings or his operatic arias to the voice," there is also a certain lapse
in logic. The works for the piano did not have the same claim to their medium
as the works Mozart composed for strings and the voice. The latter encompass

established, though varying, means of expression and repertoire. Yet, what could be more congenial than the very works that, in fact, defined and expanded the rising literature of the piano with examples of unsurpassed beauty? Mozart composed them prodigiously. In truth, he not only adapted himself to a pianistic manner but essentially formed it.

✳

Mozart's early keyboard works must be seen against the background of the extended travels of the Mozart family. They begin with the family's trips to Munich and Vienna in 1762. These were, however, only preparatory to the grand tour that commenced in June 1763 and lasted three and a half years. It took the Mozart family, with Wolfgang and his sister Marianne—Nannerl—as principal performers to Munich, Schwetzingen, Brussels, Paris, London, The Hague, Versailles, and Zurich. A second visit to Vienna took place in 1767, and the family remained there for over a year. In late 1769, Leopold Mozart took his son on the first of the important tours of Italy. There were intermittent returns to Salzburg, the last Italian sojourn ending in 1773.

The effect and influence of these travels cannot be weighed heavily enough. Mozart's perspective was immensely broadened. Most important with regard to his musical development were his performances at the courts and musical centers of Europe, appearances that brought him into contact not only with the outstanding music patrons but also with the outstanding musicians of the time. What an experience, for instance, for the young Mozart and his sister to play a concerto for two keyboards written by the Imperial Music Master Georg Christoph Wagenseil before the Viennese court of Maria Theresia in 1762, with the composer himself turning pages for the children. Just a year earlier, Mozart had tried his hand at some of Wagenseil's little clavier pieces, the learning of which was recorded by Leopold in his daughter's notebook. At Schwetzingen, the summer residence of Karl Theodor, Elector of the Palatinate, the children performed in the palace and heard the famous Mannheim orchestra.

In Brussels, the Mozarts met with Johann Gottfried Eckard—like Leopold, originally from Augsburg but by then established in Paris—whose *Six Sonates pour le clavecin*, as Wyzewa and Saint-Foix have pointed out, left their influence on Mozart.[2] The result was Mozart's Op. 1—his first published work—dedicated to Princesse Victoire, a daughter of the French monarch, and entitled *Sonates pour le Clavecin, Qui peuvent se jouer avec l'Accompagnement de Violon* (K. 6 and K. 7). An effusive dedication was written by Baron Melchior von Grimm, an enthusiastic supporter of the Mozarts.

In Paris, Mozart felt again the influence of Eckard as well as that of Johann Schobert. Schobert established the custom of grouping sonatas in pairs rather than, as usual, in groups of six.[3] Mozart's Op. 1 (K. 6 and K. 7) and Op. 2 (K. 8 and K. 9), were both printed at Paris in the spring of 1764. These sonatas show a scoring established at the time that reverses the situation of the solo sonata of the Baroque: the keyboard now becomes the expressive exponent. The optional addition of a violin part had been popular in Paris since about 1760, serving the double purpose of enriching the sonority and providing commercial advantage. That the keyboard part maintained the focus in these compositions is revealed in the origins of K. 6, a work first conceived for keyboard alone.

This sonata—its various movements found throughout the "Nannerl Notebook"—has a complicated history, the first movement having been composed at Brussels in October 1763 (before the Mozarts left for France), the second minuet having originated prior to the family's arrival in Paris in the late fall of 1763. The last movement, Allegro molto, was composed in Paris either in December 1763 or in the following January and does not appear in the notebook.[4] The violin part was added in Paris by Wolfgang himself. (This is significant because often the optional part for keyboard sonatas was provided by the publisher.) That the child made the addition is clear from the contents of a letter written by Leopold to his Salzburg friend and neighbor Lorenz Hagenauer, in which Leopold notes that he had corrected some parallel fifths in his son's violin part only to see them reinserted by the publisher.[5] With regard to this added part, Schobert's influence again surfaces: "The violin part clearly shows features which are typical of Schobert and his imitators. It is restricted among other things primarily to note-repetitions, long-held notes, doubling at the third, sixth or octave below, broken chords (sometimes with a rhythm independent of the keyboard part.)"[6]

A famous letter written by Leopold on 1 February 1764 details some particulars of the musical climate in Paris.

> The whole of French music is not worth a sou. . . . The Germans are taking the lead in the publication of their compositions. . . . Among these, Schobert, Eckard, Honauer for the clavier, and Hochbrucker and Mayr for the harp are the favorites. M. LeGrand, a French clavier player, has abandoned his own style completely and his own sonatas are now in our style. Schobert, Eckard, LeGrand and Hochbrucker have all brought us their engraved sonatas and presented them to my children.[7]

Mozart paid special homage to this group of German composers active at Paris when three years later (during the summer of 1767) he wrote several concertos, generally referred to as the *Pasticcio* Concertos, consisting of arrangements of their compositions. The following list shows the various sources and their disposition among the four concertos.[8]

	1st mvt.	2d mvt.	3d mvt.
K. 37 in F Major	Allegro Raupach Op.1, No.5 1st mvt.	Andante Unknown possibly Mozart	Rondo Honauer Op. 2, No.3 1st mvt.
K. 39 in B-flat Major	Allegro spiritoso Raupach Op.1, No. 1 1st mvt.	Andante Schobert Op. 17, No. 2	Molto Allegro Raupach Op. 1, No. 1 3d mvt
K. 40 in D Major	Allegro maestoso Honauer Op. 2, No. 1 1st mvt.	Andante Eckard Op. 1, No.4 single mvt work	Presto C. P. E. Bach La Boehmer Wq. 117
K. 41 in G Major	Allegro Honauer Op. 1, No. 1 1st mvt.	Andante Raupach Op. 1, No. 1 2d mvt.	Molto Allegro Honauer Op. 1, No. 1 3d mvt.

As seen here, a sonata movement from Eckard's Op. I forms the second movement in Mozart's Concerto in D Major K. 40. The influence of Eckard's first collection of sonatas has already been noted in connection with Mozart's Op. 1. It is of interest that Eckard's *Six Sonates pour le clavecin* (issued in 1763) appeared with an advertisement to the effect that these sonatas were also intended for performance on the clavichord and on the piano and that for this reason dynamic directions, for example, *aussi souvent les doux, et les fort*, were added.[9] It is the first suggestion of a pianistic idiom in the French keyboard literature. F. E. Kirby, in his *Short History of Keyboard Music*, asserts that in view of his dynamic markings, Eckard might be understood as having written his works specifically with the Stein piano in mind.[10] If prompted by the Augsburg musical instrument builder Johann Andreas Stein, Eckard was probably writing for a type of clavichord; in the early 1760s, Stein was still experimenting with various hybrids of keyboard instruments. Stein and Eckard were friends from Augsburg days, and Stein had visited Eckard in Paris in 1759 (the Mozarts had purchased a practice keyboard instrument, a clavichord, from Stein at Augsburg in 1763). Nonetheless, there is evidence that instruments of the new fortepiano construction were available in Paris at the time, which might have prompted Eckard's compositions as well as the advertisement.

These four concertos are of interest for yet another reason. From the evidence presented by the autographs, Eduard Reeser, editor of these works in the *Neue Mozart-Ausgabe* (hereafter referred to as *NMA*), and Wolfgang Plath, general editor of the series, have concluded that the compositions are the joint work of father and son. The works were Mozart's first venture into the concerto genre, and they reflect his earliest realization of a principle that was to assume singular importance in his oeuvre. It is understandable that Leopold wanted to guide his son in this first effort. Reeser also suggests the possibility that an imminent performance may have prompted the expedient of Leopold's guidance,[11] but Wolfgang doubtless took active part in the process of transcription.

*

Like Paris, London was one of the eighteenth-century centers with a cultural richness that must have left a deep impression upon the young visitor. Here Mozart met with a lasting musical influence through his remarkable encounter with Johann Christian Bach, the youngest of the Bach sons: "There exists between Johann Christian Bach and Mozart, to use lightly a term from Leibniz's philosophy, a wondrous kinship of souls. Also a similarity of education, the mixture of northern and southern elements."[12] The depth of their warm friendship established during the London visit is evident from Mozart's letter to his father written some fourteen years later, at St. Germain, on 27 August 1778: "Mr. Bach from London has been here for the last fortnight. . . . I love him (as you know) and respect him with all my heart; and as for him, there is no doubt that he has praised me warmly, not only to my face, but to others also, and in all seriousness—not with the exaggerated manner which some affect."[13] Also recorded are the details of their meetings during 1764–65, in Baron von Grimm's "Correspondance littéraire": "In London Bach took him between his knees and they played alternately on the same keyboard for two hours together extempore, before the King and Queen."[14] In the fall of 1769, the English philosopher Daines Barrington submitted to the Royal Society a famous report that contains the following: "The facts which I have been mentioning I was myself an eyewitness of; to which I must add, that I have been informed by two or three able musicians, when Bach the celebrated composer had begun a fugue and left off abruptly, that little Mozart hath immediately taken it up, and worked it after a most masterly manner."[15]

Throughout the London sojourn Bach, as Music Master to the Queen, was in charge of Mozart's appearances at the English court. But more important than the personal influence was his musical influence upon Mozart, as Charles Sanford Terry, the J. C. Bach biographer, has pointed out:

> From him and Manzuoli [the famous castrato] Mozart learnt the secrets of vocal technique. The later symphonies he composed in London were directly inspired by Bach's. . . . If less permanent, Bach's influence also affected Mozart's instrumental style, conveying the characteristics of his own—an almost feminine sweetness; and in his *Andantes* a rare and spontaneous beauty. Elegant rather than profound, Bach's effects were gained in large measure by the contrasts Burney observed as distinctive of his style—the alternation of *forte* and *piano*, transmission of a subject from one instrument to another, and, in general, a happy mixture of plan and improvisation.[16]

In a letter to Lorenz Hagenauer written in London and on 28 May 1764, Leopold Mozart commented that what Wolfgang knew when they left Salzburg "is a mere shadow compared with what he knows now. It exceeds all that one can imagine. He greets you from the clavier, where at the moment he is seated, playing through Kapellmeister Bach's trio."[17] (The work referred to was one of the trios from Bach's Op. 2.)

✳

While in London, Mozart wrote six sonatas, published as his Op. 3 (K. 10–15) for piano, violin (or flute), and violoncello. These were dedicated to the queen, entitled *Six Sonates pour le Clavecin qui peuvent se jouer avec l'accompagnement de Violon, ou Flûte Traversière et d'un Violoncelle*, and printed by Williamson in Thrift Street, Soho. Another edition published at the same time failed to mention the cello, and at that point began the confusion regarding the exact genre these sonatas represent. In the *NMA,* these works have been reappraised and assigned to their logical stylistic place.

> The old Mozart edition placed them unthinkingly in the category of violin-piano sonatas. The NMA, on the other hand, has included them intentionally in the volume of piano trios, for these works in fact mark the historical point at which the piano trio, and the piano sonata which is merely accompanied diverge as musical forms. . . . The addition of the violoncello places the six sonatas in a midway position as regards musical form; on the one hand they are structurally conceived as keyboard sonatas with an ad libitum accompanying melodic instrument (violin or flute) and are therefore in the line with K. 6–9 and K. 26–31—in this case the inclusion of the violoncello part is to be regarded as being purely incidental and as evidence of ad libitum practice, and it may be taken as at least perfectly feasible in opera I, II and IV. On the other hand, the very fact that a musical practice which is self-evident through the addition of an especially printed violoncello part that does

not just double the keyboard bass throughout, makes the sonatas K. 10–15 of special interest in the history of the musical form. The six sonatas mark the first step
in the transition from the keyboard sonatas accompanied ad libitum to the later
classical piano trio.[18]

As a document from the London period, the "London Notebook" presents
us with a collection of pieces by the seven-year-old that complete the impression of Mozart's earliest keyboard idiom. In the *NMA*, this collection is issued
together with the well-known notebook for Mozart's sister that, in fact, includes the very first compositions ascribed to Mozart (K. 1–5).[19] Since the
manuscript shows, once again, predominantly Leopold's hand, we cannot be
sure to what extent we are dealing with Mozart's own work. A third collection, described as Leopold's notebook for Wolfgang, has been proved by
Wolfgang Plath to be a forgery.[20]

Possibly only in part made up of genuine clavier pieces and in part of arrangements, these collections represent a keyboard style that has already
moved away from the typical harpsichord writing. Octave doublings for the
left hand and chord figurations for the right and left hands suggest the rising
symphonic age: the prevalent style of composition is no longer entirely com-
patible with the nature of the harpsichord.

Besides the sonatas, K. 10–15, and the London Notebook, K. Anh. 109b
(15a–55), three other works emanate from the London sojourn: the three concertos, K. 107 (21b), based on sonatas by J. C. Bach. Written a number of
years later—not before 1770, as Wolfgang Plath has shown—these concertos
are arrangements of three of Bach's six sonatas composed in the 1760s and
published in 1768 in London with the title *Six Sonatas for the Pianoforte or Harpsichord*. Unlike the *Pasticcio* Concertos, these arrangements are adaptations of
complete works—sonatas two, three, and four of Bach's Op. 5—and maintain the original scheme of movements and key. Detailed analysis of the
manuscripts (also undertaken by Plath) show that these concertos, like the
earlier arrangements, represent the joint efforts of father and son. The respective handwritings indicate, however, that while Leopold transferred the keyboard part, adding a figured bass, the more original task of adding the strings
was left to Wolfgang.[21]

The scant scoring (two violins and a bass) has given rise to the argument—
introduced by Wyzewa and Saint-Foix—that these concertos are "primitive."
As Reeser has pointed out, it is an argument that cannot be maintained.[22] We
are concerned with an established pattern of orchestration, widely represented
in the piano concertos of the time as well as in the early symphonic masses
and the other works for the Catholic service (the so-called Viennese string
trio), and the addition of the string parts involved significant structural

changes in these particular works. Nor is the part-writing less deft than in the *Pasticcio* Concertos that included woodwinds and, in K. 40, even trumpets.

Most important are the interpolations made by Mozart in the initial tutti sections of the concertos, especially in the second and third concertos. Obviously, Mozart's handling of the opening material shows originality, but more significantly it suggests an assimilation and development of J. C. Bach's nascent thematic dualism, a structural characteristic that was to become assured in Mozart's later style.[23] In the second and third concertos (G major and E-flat major, respectively), Mozart begins merely with the opening material found in the original exposition. He reserves the second theme, chosen from the original sonata, for the piano exposition, also a frequent feature of his later concertos. Mozart's skill of invention as well as in handling given material becomes evident in the course of these arrangements. Even in the first concerto (in D major), where thematic dualism arises from the inherent contrast of original themes, the comparison of original and transcription is rendered all the more striking through Mozart's part-writing and articulation and dynamic indications.

As described, the title page of J. C. Bach's Op. 5, the source of Mozart's concertos, indicates performance on either the piano or harpsichord. The conventions of the time suggest a casual approach to performance requirements; furthermore, eighteenth-century publishers addressed themselves for commercial considerations to both progressive and conservative customers.[24] J. C. Bach as a young "progressive" was an advocate of the piano. He is traditionally cited as being the first to have given a public piano concert in London—in 1768 on an instrument made at the workshop of Johannes Zumpe.[25] It is particularly interesting that Op. 5 contains dynamic markings throughout that could only be carried out on the piano (the first sonatas even contain the marking *crescendo*). Mozart met in these compositions a style congenial to his sensitivity; and it is significant that the impressions he gained from J. C. Bach's keyboard compositions were inextricably linked to the new instrument.

On their return from London, the Mozarts stopped at The Hague where Wolfgang wrote a new set of *Sonates pour le Clavecin avec L'Accompagnement d'un Violon*, dedicated to Princess Caroline of Nassau-Weilburg. The large-scale design is on the whole more casual, following largely a two-movement scheme favored by J. C. Bach. Mozart was recovering from a severe illness that may have contributed to his more limited involvement with this series than with the earlier works of the kind.

Yet the texture of these sonatas draws new attention to the role of the clavier. Though the nature of the violin part has not essentially changed, that of the keyboard part has. Here, for instance, is Mozart's first use of the technique of crossed hands, and it occurs for patently stylistic reasons. Unlike similar instances in Scarlatti's writing or the crossing of entirely polyphonic parts in J. S. Bach's works, Mozart's recourse to the device suggests a keyboard idiom formed by the new orchestral practices. It is needed to free the left hand for chordal patterns that sustain dramatic tension (an early example, but of lesser significance, occurs in the London Notebook, where the hands cross merely in sharing an arpeggio).

Two sets of variations were published in Holland, the eight variations on a Dutch song K. 24 and the seven variations on the old national anthem, *Willem van Nassau,* K. 25. They were composed during the late winter of 1766 and issued in connection with the celebrations surrounding the installation of Prince William V as sovereign ruler. Throughout the journeys, Mozart routinely offered examples of his art in improvisation, as was common in eighteenth-century performances. Owing to the festive circumstances of the installation, we encounter the first published sets of variations, which indeed might be considered a written record of improvisation. Common themes for variations included opera arias or songs; others might be marches or minuets. In short, the source was popular, widely known, giving the cultivated listener the pleasure of following the transformations while presenting a challenge to the performer's skill and imagination.

Both sets of variations end with conspicuous use of the "Alberti bass," a device that had already figured prominently in Mozart's sonatas and would become one of Mozart's favored forms of accompaniment. Its typical pattern of broken chords—attributed to the invention of Domenico Alberti, an Italian singer, composer, and harpsichordist of the early eighteenth century[26]—was well suited to sustaining harmonies. And because of the piano's singular ability to impart an expressive quality to repetitive patterns, the Alberti bass eventually proved to be a preferred feature of piano music. As we shall see, Mozart was fully to develop the expressive possibilities of this accompanimental formula.

As documents of Mozart's improvisational skill, the two sets of variations suggest above all his prodigious gift as a performer. An elaborate account of Mozart's keyboard technique comes from Baron von Grimm.

True prodigies are sufficiently rare to be worth speaking of, when you have had the occasion to see one. A Kapellmeister of Salzburg, Mozart by name, has just arrived here with two children who cut the prettiest figures in the world. His daughter, eleven years of age, plays the harpsichord in the most brilliant manner; she performs the longest and most difficult pieces with an astonishing precision. Her brother, who will be seven years old next February, is such an extraordinary phenomenon that one is hard put to it to believe what one sees with one's eyes and hears with one's ears. It means little for this child to perform with the greatest precision the most difficult pieces, with hands that can hardly stretch a sixth; but what is really incredible is to see him improvise for an hour on end and in so doing give rein to the imagination of his genius and to a mass of enchanting ideas, which moreover he knows how to connect with taste and without confusion. The most consummate Kapellmeister should not be more profound than he in the science of harmony and modulations, which he knows how to connect by the least expected but always accurate paths. He has such great familiarity with the keyboard that when it is hidden from him by a cloth spread over it, he plays on this cloth with the same speed and with the same precision.[27]

Leopold had originally planned to take his family to Italy, through Milan and Venice, as part of the journey commenced in 1763. While still in England, however, the Mozarts were approached repeatedly by the Dutch envoy who, on behalf of Princess Caroline of Nassau-Weilburg, implored the family to visit Holland. Persuaded to detour, they were warmly received. The interest of the Princess was genuine and well founded. Her mother was Princess Anne (the daughter of George II of England) who, as a personal student of Handel, had demonstrated an unusual musical gift. The stay in the Netherlands disrupted the Mozarts' schedule, and the long-awaited visit to Italy did not occur until 1769. Eventually, there were three Italian trips but they were markedly different from the earlier ones. Mozart, by now an adolescent, was subjected to a number of decisive new impressions. He was in the land of opera; the secrets of the contrapuntal art were opened to him; and he met with demonstrations of vocal virtuosity unique to Italian singers. Virtuosity now became an integral element of his style, one that made itself strongly felt as technical brilliance increasingly characterized his performance as a keyboard artist.

His appearances gained him a diploma from the Accademia Filarmonica of Bologna and a Papal appointment as a Knight of the Golden Order. A program preserved from Mozart's concert at Mantua in January 1770 characteristically documents a new range of achievements.[28] It began with the sight-reading of a concerto and a sonata, after which Mozart transposed the sonata to a different key. He also improvised a set of variations and a sonata, the themes of which were given to him by the concertmaster of the orchestra. The concert culminated in the extemporaneous composition and performance of a fugue, again on a theme submitted to him, "which he brought to such a masterly harmonic interweaving of all the parts and so bold a resolution as to leave the hearers astounded."[29]

✶

Prophetically, this finale of a bravura performance suggests a confluence of stylistic elements that, at the height of his creative career, Mozart brought to perfection in his pianistic writing. It was unusual enough for a concert artist of the time to choose a fugue as the conclusion of an appearance—fugal art was generally at its lowest ebb—but the "masterly harmonic interweaving of all the parts" was to take on new and ever different dimensions that characterized his pianistic oeuvre at the crowning of his lifework.

2

Mozart and the Transformation of Keyboard Practice

∗

The account of Mozart's contrapuntal feat at Mantua suggests an aspect of his art that is generally unfamiliar: from an early age he showed an interest in the celebrated traditions of organ improvisation. "Mozart's command of the art of organ playing was formed by his experiences throughout the European countries. . . . In his knowledge of the great organs of Europe and of the different style of performance associated with them, Mozart was second to none, not even to Bach and Handel."[1] Though Hanns Dennerlein's statement loses some of its weight when one considers the extent of Mozart's travels, there is no question about Mozart's mastery of the organ. "He played so splendidly on the King's organ that they all value his organ-playing more highly than his clavier playing," wrote Leopold about the child's performances at the English court.[2] In 1777 Mozart commented to Johann Stein, the famous instrument builder of Augsburg, that the organ was his favorite instrument. During this Augsburg visit, Mozart gave a performance that he described in detail to his father:

> Then the others whispered to the Dean that he should just hear me play something in the organ style. I asked him to give me a theme. He declined, but one of the monks gave me one. I put it through its paces and in the middle (the fugue was in G minor) I started off in the key and played something quite lively, though in the same tempo; and after that the theme over again, but this time arseways. Finally it occurred to me, could I not use my lively tune as the theme for a fugue? I did not waste much time in asking, but did so at once, and it went as neatly as if Daser [a Salzburg tailor] had fitted it. The Dean was absolutely staggered "Why, it's simply phenomenal, that's all I can say," he said. "I should never have believed what I have heard. You are a first-rate fellow. My Abbot told me, it is true, that he had never heard anyone play the organ so smoothly and so soundly."[3]

Leopold, himself a skilled organist, had played at the same monastery as a young man.

During another Augsburg performance, one which included the concerto for three claviers, Mozart "then played another solo, quite in the style of the organ."[4] The quotation illustrates that Mozart clearly distinguished among the different styles of keyboard performance and that he, who had a phenomenal facility in all keyboard styles, embraced a distinct organ style with its learned connotations. Yet this has also given rise to the assertion that certain polyphonically oriented piano compositions were intended to be organ pieces. Dennerlein, in discussing Mozart's works for organ, claims that a C Minor Fantasy (evidently the one that has long been associated with the Piano Sonata K. 457) was originally conceived to preface a fugue for organ.[5] Mozart wrote two Fantasies in C Minor—K. 396 (385f) in 1782 and K. 475 in 1785, the latter of which the Viennese publisher Artaria eventually published with the Sonata K. 457 (also in C minor and composed a year earlier) as Mozart's Op. 11. Unfortunately, Dennerlein does not specify to which of the two fantasies in C minor he refers, though he asserts that the general style of the fantasy and the fact that the work's autograph is concluded on the dominant suggest the possibility that it might indeed have been intended as the prelude to a polyphonic work that was never completed or has since been lost. One can infer from the context of his discussion that his reference must be to the earlier of the two fantasies, K. 396 (385f), which was in fact left incomplete by Mozart and which was finished by Maximilian Stadler; however, Mozart's autograph of this work concludes on the relative major, E-flat major, and not on the dominant.[6] The autographs to the Fantasy in C Minor K. 475 and the Sonata in C Minor K. 457, long considered to be lost, were discovered in 1990 at a seminary in Philadelphia and are now in the collections of the International Mozart Foundation in Salzburg. The autograph to the C Minor Fantasy K. 475, although markedly different in certain details from the first published edition and all subsequent editions, including the *NMA* publication (Serie IX/ 25/2, 1986), concludes in C minor.

The organ continued to claim a place in Mozart's professional life. After his early spectacular performances, he attempted to secure positions as a court or cathedral organist in France. His first and only notable appointment was that of cathedral organist at Salzburg. Even later in Vienna, he was considered an organ expert, and he was chosen for the position of Kapellmeister at St. Stephan's, which he was never in fact to assume. In mentioning the document of appointment that Mozart received, Georg Nikolaus von Nissen in his *Biographie W. A. Mozarts* recorded his recollection of the words of the dying composer: "Just now I must go when I could have lived in peace! Now that I would no longer have to be a slave . . . of fashion . . . I must take leave of my art."[7]

✳

Throughout the eighteenth century, a shift in public performance took place—from the church to the public concert hall. The organ retained its established claim to the solo role, but the piano was to become its unequivocal counterpart as a solo instrument in modern public performance. This development is marked by a somewhat transitory phase in the harpsichord's history, for as soon as this instrument assumed a modern solo function in recital or orchestral concert, it also became the subject of "improvements" by which its nature was essentially changed. In a recent study, Eva Badura-Skoda advances the interesting thesis that the harpsichord concertos from Bach's later years in Leipzig were actually performed on an early type of fortepiano.

It must be remembered that the harpsichord entered public performance through the rise of opera. It served an all-important role as the conductor's instrument but nonetheless an accompanying role, not as a solo instrument. True, a solo literature had developed for the instrument in the private domain of the home and princely chamber. Early collections, such as those compiled for the use of English nobility, the *Fitzwilliam Virginal Book* or *Parthenia,* "the first musicke that ever was printed for the Virginalls," were intended, as the titles indicate, for a small variety of the instrument. But even the large gravicembalo remained, as a solo instrument, the instrument of *musica da camera.* And at its culmination—in the works of the French clavecinists, of Domenico Scarlatti, and of Handel and Bach—the solo literature for the harpsichord was addressed to private entertainment or instruction.

The harpsichord's role as the continuo instrument of chamber music, however, began to vary during the eighteenth century. Handel designates the title of some of his Opus I sonatas *"a Flauto e Cembalo,"* now distinguishing a "thorough bass for the harpsichord or violoncello." In Bach's and Telemann's chamber music, the harpsichord assumes at times an obbligato function equaling that of the solo part, the new integral role foreshadowing the role of the piano in the late chamber duos and trios.

A similar process led to the emergence of the keyboard concerto derived from the concerto grosso and the early violin concerto. In elevating the harpsichord to a *concertino* instrument in the Fifth Brandenburg Concerto, Bach is traditionally considered to have provided the first example of the solo keyboard concerto. Bach's early period coincided with the decisive rise of the solo concerto and the primacy of the violin. Against this background, Bach's "creation" of the keyboard concerto as a type seems doubly interesting, though it did not immediately challenge the hegemony of the violin: Bach's later keyboard concertos are predominantly transcriptions of earlier violin compositions. But whereas the primary instrumental exponent of the Baroque was the violin, the keyboard instrument was to dominate a later era of the concerto.

Gradually freed from its continuo function, the keyboard instrument became the principal solo instrument in the concerto just at the time the concerto entered public concert life, and with this development coincided the change from harpsichord to piano. Nonetheless, the Italian word *cembalo*, like its German counterpart, *Klavier*, remained a generic term for keyboard instruments, and this usage extended into the early nineteenth century. Beethoven, in his Sonata Op. 101—a work expressly written for the hammerklavier—supplies the direction *Tutto il cembalo ma piano*.[8]

It was somewhat in the sense of stating an issue that in 1788, the last year of his life, C. P. E. Bach wrote a double concerto for harpsichord and piano. Placing the two keyboard instruments side by side and exploiting the unique timbre of each instrument, the work, rather than stressing particular idiomatic writing, stresses the differences in sonority—though not the characteristic advantages of each keyboard mechanism. Written by a composer who was the unquestioned authority on contemporary keyboard practice, the concerto nonetheless points out the role that the piano had begun to assume.

The works of Johann Christian Bach further document a shift in emphasis. His early compositions designate the harpsichord, but in his Op. 5 and Op. 7—sets of sonatas and concertos, respectively—the titles read "for the Pianoforte or Harpsichord." While the dual designation was to continue for some time for commercial reasons, the keyboard style of J. C. Bach, the "incomparable melodist,"[9] serves as a reminder that he was the composer who introduced the new instrument to the public.

But Mozart's keyboard works, the compositions from his childhood and adolescence aside, were composed for the piano: "It should be noted that he wrote for the same instrument as Beethoven, Weber, or Chopin—not for the clavichord or the harpsichord, but for the pianoforte, although of course not for the powerful instrument we know in the products of Erard or Steinway."[10] To this unequivocal statement with which he introduces the chapter "The Clavier" in his Mozart biography, Alfred Einstein adds the fine point that one must not be confused by the fact that a famous harpsichordist (he refers to Wanda Landowska) gains ovations by playing the *Rondo alla turca* from the A Major Sonata "on his or her instrument." Nathan Broder (in his article "Mozart and the 'Clavier'") has discussed in detail the point at which Mozart appears to have begun composing exclusively with the piano in mind.[11] Broder specifies the end of 1777 as the date but admits that even the set of sonatas for keyboard solo, written almost three years earlier, suggest the piano.

✴

The invention of the piano mechanism is credited to Bartolomeo Cristo-fori, instrument maker at the court of the Medici in Florence, in a document mentioning the year 1698 that describes the new possibilities of obtaining a softer or stronger tone by the degree of pressure applied to the key.[12] By 1721, Jean Marius in Paris and Christoph Gottlieb Schröter in Dresden had experi-mented with instruments for which the chief active component was a hammer rather than the quill, although it must be remembered that the new instrument arose from the harpsichord ateliers, because a keyboard action with greater *piano e forte* possibilities was sought. After Cristofori's essential and far-reach-ing advancements of the piano mechanism, the instrument developed mostly at the hands of the German makers Gottfried Silbermann and, later, Johann Andreas Stein. Another German instrument maker, Johannes Zumpe, immi-grated to England in the middle of the century and settled in London. As mentioned earlier, it was on a Zumpe piano that J. C. Bach played during the celebrated concert of 1768. Another immigrant, the Swiss Burkart Tschudi, opened an establishment that ultimately developed into the Broadwood firm, which was to provide Beethoven with a favorite instrument—though Bee-thoven's ultimate preference seems to have been the pianos made by the Vien-nese firm of Stein-Streicher.[13]

Thus the piano emerged from the workshops of harpsichord builders. Cris-tofori called his instrument *gravicembalo col piano e forte* and Marius referred to his instrument as a *clavecin à mallets*. Tschudi had established himself as one of the finest builders of harpsichords in Europe, and yet the eventual decline of the harpsichord was bound up with the very improvements that sought to adapt it to the demands and expectations of a new age of music.

In the 1760s, Tschudi had developed devices designed to increase the harpsi-chord's expressive powers and provide it with a wide and changeable dynamic range. One device, the Venetian swell (patented in 1769) consisted of a set of louvers laid over the strings of the instrument (in the manner of an inner lid) and controlled by a mechanism of two pedals, which, when engaged, varied the positions of the louvers from closed to open.[14] Mozart played on a compa-rable instrument during the summer of 1765, an instrument that was one of four Tschudi harpsichords designated for the collection of Frederick the Great. Its curious mechanism, described in the following notice and similar to the Venetian swell in purpose, must have made an impression on the young

Mozart, as it evidently did on his father, who probably wrote the advertisement:

> *London, 5 July 1765.* The very famous clavier maker Burkard Thudy [*sic*] of this city, a Swiss by birth, had the honour of making for the King of Prussia a wing-shaped instrument with two manuals which was very much admired by all who saw it. It has been regarded as particularly noteworthy that Mr. Thudy connected all the stops to a pedal, so that they can be drawn by treading, one after another, and the decrease and increase of tone may be varied at will, which *crescendo* and *decrescendo* has been long wished for by clavier players. Mr. Thudy has moreover conceived the good notion of having his extraordinary clavier played for the first time by the most extraordinary clavier player in the world, namely by the very celebrated master of music, Wolfg. Mozart, aged nine, the admirable son of the Salzburg Kapellmeister, Herr Mozart.[15]

By the 1770s, the piano had become established in major cities, and Mozart's encounter with the new instrument is variously documented. While at Munich during the winter of 1774–75 for the preparation and premiere of his opera buffa *La finta giardiniera*, Mozart took part in the city's musical life with his father. Among the activities was a clavier contest between Mozart and Ignaz von Beecke (a virtuoso and also formerly a child prodigy) held at the home of Franz Albert, who had "an excellent fortepiano in his home."[16] It was during this Munich sojourn, more specifically early in 1775, that Mozart composed his first solo sonatas for a keyboard instrument, the piano sonatas K. 279–83 (189d–h) and K. 284 (205b).

In the fall of 1777, Mozart had left Salzburg on a tour of cities in southern Germany with the hope of gaining a court appointment. After visiting Munich, the Mozarts—Wolfgang's mother accompanied him on this journey—went to Augsburg, Leopold's native city. Here Mozart met Johann Andreas Stein and played upon the latter's pianos. Mozart's enthusiastic reaction to Stein's pianos prompted the detailed, and celebrated, letter to his father:

> This time I must begin at once with Stein's pianofortes. Before I had seen any of his make, Späth's claviers had always been my favorites. But now I much prefer Stein's, for they damp ever so much better than the Regensburg instruments. When I strike strongly, no matter whether I leave the finger down or lift it, the tone essentially ceases the moment I let it be heard. In whatever way I touch the keys, the tone is always even. It never jars, it is never stronger or weaker or entirely absent; in a word, it is always even. It is true that he does not sell a pianoforte of this kind for less than three hundred gulden, but the trouble and labour which Stein puts into the making of it cannot be paid for. . . . His instruments have the special advantage over others that they are made with escape action. Only one maker in a hundred bothers about this. But without an escapement it is impossible to avoid

jangling and vibration after the note is struck. When you touch the keys, the hammers fall back again the moment after they have struck the strings, whether you hold down the keys or release them. . . . Here and at Munich I played all my six sonatas by heart several times [the previously mentioned sonatas composed at Munich in 1775]. I played the fifth, in G, at the grand concert in the Stube. The last one in D, sounds exquisite on Stein's pianoforte. The device too which you work with your knee [the damper mechanism] is better on his than on other instruments. I have only to touch it and it works; and when you shift your knee the slightest bit, you do not hear the least reverberation.[17]

As the letter illustrates, Mozart was thoroughly acquainted with the instrument of the principal piano makers in southern Germany. His understanding of the instrument was complete, including all aspects of its technical mechanisms and its physical construction. While in Augsburg, he had the opportunity to play on several Stein products, organs, and clavichords as well as pianos, and as his letters to his father show, he was thoroughly impressed. Due to the propitious availability of three Stein pianos during the Augsburg visit, a performance of Mozart's Concerto for Three Claviers K. 242 (composed in 1776) took place in which Mozart, Stein, and Johann Michael Demmler, the Augsburg cathedral organist, figured as soloists. In fact, even before Wolfgang's birth, Archbishop Sigismund von Schrattenbach, who eventually became Mozart's first employer, possessed a piano made by Stein, an instrument on which Mozart presumably played during the years he served as concertmaster and organist in Salzburg.[18]

✳

While the invention and improvement of the piano mechanism, through refinements intended for the harpsichord, are clearly documented, the evolution in keyboard idiom accompanying the shift in musical expression and taste is less immediately apparent. The change was both subtle and complex, and like many changes of such significance, it was rooted in the artistic achievements of previous generations.

In 1747 J. S. Bach visited, as we know, the court of Frederick the Great upon an invitation extended through the conductor of royal chamber music, Bach's son Carl Philipp Emanuel. The young Prussian monarch's keen interest in music—he was an amateur flutist and a composer of some skill—variously manifested itself, in particular in an outstanding collection of musical instruments among which were four harpsichords by Burkart Tschudi and more than seven pianos from Silbermann's workshop. Silbermann had improved his instruments significantly since 1726, when J. S. Bach first reacted rather indifferently to them.[19] It was on such a greatly improved instrument, and in the sense of proudly exhibiting his collection, that at their famous meeting Frederick supplied a theme and asked his guest to improvise a fugue, and the work with which Bach obliged appeared eventually as the three-part ricercare of the *Musical Offering*.

In addition to this and the trio sonata, and the canonic settings, the *Musical Offering* contains the well-known six-part ricercare, which forms a remarkable companion to the three-part work. Christoph Wolff has pointed out that distinct stylistic idioms in the two ricercari call for particular keyboard performance, dispelling an earlier, generally held notion that considered the works in completely abstract terms and without specific assignment of instrument.[20] Certain stylistic features of writing in the three-part ricercare clearly suggest an intention of performance on the piano. Wolff mentions both in connection with the three-part ricercare and the trio sonata from the *Musical Offering*, a particular gesture on Bach's part to his son's style, and it is important to remember that it was the medium of the pianoforte that inspired the composition in the first place. The argument is strengthened by our knowledge that J. S. Bach was in this period sufficiently impressed with Silbermann's product to act as his sales agent in Leipzig.[21]

In contrast, as Wolff points out, the six-part ricercare suggests an instrumental texture germane to those instruments traditionally linked to the realization of pure polyphony—the harpsichord or organ. Unlike the three-part ricercare, the six-voice ricercare is expressly conservative in style. The traditional open-score notation resumed by Bach in this and other polyphonic works from his last years unfolds a work of majestic contrapuntal dimensions—J. S. Bach's supreme response to the Prussian monarch's theme. The stylistic contrast evident in the two ricercari illustrates the confluence of idioms prevalent by midcentury, but more significantly, it demonstrates the rise of a new expressive style and its recognition by the very composer whose work represents the culmination of Baroque keyboard art.

The invention of the piano mechanism, other technical innovations in instrument construction, and the concomitant changes in instrumental idiom were symptoms of a change in musical taste that redefined above all the significance of dynamic contrast in music. Dynamic contrast had been a salient feature of baroque music, but the music of the new era sought expansion of such contrast. Born of an age in which rationalist concerns guided views, contrast of mood and emotion gained a realistic currency. "We know how fast emotions change, since they themselves are nothing but motion and restlessness. . . . The composer then must take on a thousand characters,"[22] we find written by 1749 in *Der kritische Musikus an der Spree*, a journal edited by Friedrich Wilhelm Marpurg, the eminent theorist. Documenting this evolution in musical thought, Johann Georg Sulzer stated in a formal study of aesthetics:

> The principal, if not indeed the sole function of a perfect musical composition is the accurate expression of emotions and passions in all their varying and individual nuances. . . . Many composers have been led astray by an over-fondness for certain pleasant-sounding and skillfully-contrived formulae that express particular emotions. It should be borne in mind that such repetitions are often detrimental to expression and are suitable only for certain obsessive emotions and passions. . . . Other emotions, however, involve impressions that are constantly changing, variable and transient. In such cases, frequent reiteration of the same expressive formula is unnatural.[23]

The various dynamic refinements invented for both the harpsichord and clavichord (such as the pedals, muting stops, etc.) sought in vain to endow their respective instruments with resources to express adequately a new musical ideal. That ideal, based on immediacy of emotional expression, was more aptly reflected by an instrument construction that allowed the player the greatest freedom in playing "piano e forte."

✳

It is a fact of history that the eighteenth-century piano for which Mozart wrote was very different from its modern counterpart. Unlike the evolution undergone by the piano in the nineteenth century, developments throughout the eighteenth century were tied to experiments and rapid advancements in the designs of particular makers. Most notable were the differences between the instruments of southern German and Austrian workshops and those of the English, whose instruments offered a more resonant sound but required a heavier action. It has become commonly accepted usage, however, to designate all period instruments or their replicas in general by the adopted term *fortepiano*.

Though Mozart lavished enthusiastic praise on the instruments of Johann Andreas Stein of Augsburg, a fortepiano built by Anton Walter of Vienna and purchased by 1785 became his favorite instrument; it is preserved in the museum established at Mozart's birthplace and administered by the International Mozart Foundation, Salzburg. Typical of instrument construction of the period, the frame of Mozart's piano was made of wood, unlike nineteenth-century instruments, whose particular innovation was an iron frame capable of supporting the increased pressure of cross-stringing. The instrument's wooden hammers were covered with leather, in contrast to the use of felt in later instruments. Obviously, this feature affected the tone, imparting a quality that is gentle yet clear, transparent, and precise. In accordance with the light weight of the wooden construction are the instrument's relatively small dimensions, accommodating a compass of only five octaves, from FF to f^3. The keys are narrow and the bed of the keys shallow. In comparison with the modern piano, the sound had a more highly defined character in each register, a quality that, despite its individuality, blended with the woodwinds and strings in a manner not equaled by present-day timbres. Not only capable of sounding *piano e forte*, the instrument offered a singular range of gradations in dynamics, although its tone—highly sensitive to pressure—once produced, decayed quickly.

The instrument was equipped with two knee levers to engage the damper mechanism. The lever on the left raised all the dampers while that on the right engaged the treble part of the keyboard (beginning with c^1), so that both a wider and more precise range of coloristic effects could be gained. There was also a hand stop, the "Moderatorzug" (a moderator, also known as a "Pianozug" or celeste stop), which, when engaged, pulled forward a strip of material between the strings and hammers, muting the color of the sound. To a degree, it resembled in effect the *una corda* pedal or knee lever that shifted the hammer mechanism to the side so that only one of two or three strings was struck.[24]

As we know from his correspondence, Mozart also had a pedal board installed. It resembled the pedal board of an organ, though it rather appeared as a separate instrument, to be placed on the floor with the fortepiano resting on it. Like the organ pedal, it was played by the feet and extended the bass range of the instrument, probably covering in itself a two-octave range. While it has disappeared, it is known that Mozart employed the expanded instrument for the Vienna subscription concerto performances as well as for improvisation. Mozart probably played independent bass parts on this pedal board as well as doubling bass passages of the left hand; thus his hands were free for filling in and varying the keyboard texture. The use of the pedal board, particularly in connection with improvisation, serves as a reminder of Mozart's predilection for performing on the organ.

*

The piano's leading role was emphasized, as we have said, by its function in public concert life. Arising in part from the tradition of the *collegia musica*, in part from the need for musical performance during church seasons that precluded opera, and in part from middle-class initiative, public concerts had become established in the course of the seventeenth and eighteenth centuries. The *Concert spirituel* in Paris was the most famous of the new institutions, and its success influenced the beginnings of other public concerts throughout Europe.

The development of public concert life documented the changing role of music in society. With enlightened absolutism, a new social order had begun to make itself felt. In addition to continuing aristocratic and church patronage, an enlarged source of interest, a growing middle class, exerted its own demand for music:

> The international exchange of composers and compositions that forms the background of modern musical life started on a large scale. . . . The most significant element in this new musical life, and the one largely responsible for its intensity, was the large fraternity of musical amateurs. Composers who formerly addressed themselves exclusively to princes and archbishops, now turned to Kenner und Liebhaber, connoisseurs and amateurs.[25]

This "large fraternity of musical amateurs" who formed the modern concert audience decisively influenced the course of music in the eighteenth century. Music "for connoisseurs and amateurs" became a common formula in music publishing, distinguishing not only among intended performers but also among types of music (C. P. E. Bach's series of sonatas, fantasias, and rondos are designated *für Kenner und Liebhaber*). The piano, gaining from the heritage of private music making in earlier keyboard practice, gradually became the principal instrument of the amateur in solo and chamber music, at the same time asserting itself on the public stage through the singularly important genre of the concerto, which placed it on a par with the symphonic orchestra. The concerto came to be a customary part of the public concert, giving its very name to the event, and the composer at whose hands the classical concerto achieved consummate perfection and who, moreover, became its first supreme exponent was Mozart.

✳

There remained one keyboard instrument totally dissociated from public concert life: the clavichord. The clavichord combined the advantage of a delicate tone with a capacity, due to its unique mechanism, for the most intense expression. The tangent that strikes the string, in effect determining the pitch (somewhat in the manner of a string player's finger brought down hard on the string, without bow action), remains under the control of the performer through the medium of the key. Thus, the dynamic range and spectrum of sound can be varied at will. The prime example of a special effect produced by this action is the *Bebung* or "trembling," the unusual device of keyboard vibrato.

We know that Mozart played clavichords throughout his life. The Mozart family had purchased a traveling model for the children to use while on the concert tours of the 1760s. By 1782, after his marriage to Constanze, Mozart kept a clavichord at home for composing.[26] He maintained this instrument in addition to a piano he acquired either about the same time or in the years immediately following. The latter, however, made by the Viennese builder Anton Walter around 1780, was used for performances and thus was often absent from the household.

The clavichord enjoyed a particular popularity in central and northern Germany. Principally represented through C. P. E. Bach's work, what might be considered a special clavichord repertoire became established. Though his father had shown a fondness for the clavichord (an account of the distribution of his estate showed that he had made a present to his son Johann Christian of three clavichords, one with a set of pedals),[27] C. P. E. Bach's personal advocacy of the instrument as well as his stature in a musical world given to new tastes influenced others to cultivate a new keyboard literature. The instrument's sonority and sensitive nuance of tone made it a favored instrument of the artistic milieu in which the prevailing aesthetic ideal came to be the *empfindsame Stil.*

*

The period of Mozart's life is spanned by two treatises on keyboard playing, C. P. E. Bach's *Versuch über die wahre Art das Clavier zu spielen* (1753) and Daniel Gottlob Türk's *Klavierschule* (1789).[28] C. P. E. Bach's *Essay* is of fundamental importance, and its direct influence is still evident in Türk's discussion. Türk's contribution is uniquely comprehensive, gaining from its perspective on keyboard developments at the end of the century. Both studies share and exemplify contemporary didactic thought in their patent focus on the clavichord. Because its action was the most sensitive, the clavichord was the instrument singled out for the discussion of keyboard technique. Though C. P. E. Bach noted the piano's distinctive qualities and considered it favorably in his discussion ("The pianoforte and clavichord provide the best accompaniment in performance that require the most elegant taste"), the clavichord retained priority ("It is at the clavichord that a keyboardist may be most exactly evaluated").[29] Türk was no less emphatic and maintained that "the proper klavier or clavichord still has particular superiority over the majority of keyboard instruments" (Türk designates the harpsichord invariably as *Flügel*).[30]

The studies consider various aspects of keyboard performance and technique. However, C. P. E. Bach and Türk weigh their discussions differently. Though Türk devotes a substantial portion of his treatise to a detailed discussion of embellishments, his greatest contribution deals with fingering. In contrast to C. P. E. Bach's single though substantial chapter on fingering, Türk's discussion of the subject is in five distinct sections. His study opens with a chapter devoted to the basic elements of music and closes with a chapter on interpretation and execution (performance).[31] C. P. E. Bach lends considerable emphasis to thorough-bass accompaniment as well as to solo performance, and he presents a detailed discussion of ornamentation. In much the same manner that Türk's consideration of fingering offers comment on the advancements made in keyboard technique during the late eighteenth century, C. P. E. Bach's focus on accompaniment stands as an artistic summary of the continuo practice.

C. P. E. Bach's *Versuch* has been acknowledged through the ages as providing the foundation of modern keyboard technique. Referring to his father's principles of fingering, he introduces the use of the thumb; but while in general his fingerings for scales provide a basis for the modern pianistic technique, certain ones suggest a characteristic clavichord orientation. The crossing of the third finger over the fourth or of the fourth over the fifth and vice versa in scale passages, the repeated use of the second and fourth or the second and third fingers in passages of thirds, the use of the same finger on successive slurred notes, and fingerings that suggest inordinate stretches by modern comparison all derived from C. P. E. Bach's inclination toward an instrument whose nature and construction (the narrow, closely spaced keys) facilitated such patterns.[32]

Türk provides extensive fingering for patterns including a wide range of intervals, for passage work characterized by leaps, and for patterns consisting of two and three parts to be played in one hand. Moreover, he considers the most advantageous positions for the hands in passages in which they must alternate, cross, or play intertwined. In short, Türk discusses all aspects of keyboard technique, concluding with illustrative examples ranging from a patently idiomatic keyboard style to an adapted symphonic style. Throughout the study, Türk demonstrates a thorough acquaintance with the different national keyboard styles. In the chapter on performance, he devotes discussion, as had C. P. E. Bach, to the expressive feature of *Bebung* as a nuance in sound unique to the clavichord. However, he assigns to an appendix the description of characteristically pianistic patterns—the Alberti bass and broken octaves (Murky bass)—while stressing them as essential to keyboard playing.[33]

As we know, Türk studied C. P. E. Bach's *Versuch* thoroughly, and in the preface to his work he acknowledges formally and respectfully his indebtedness. The influence of C. P. E. Bach is seen throughout Türk's manual, and

C. P. E. Bach is specifically cited in numerous references and comparisons. The significance of C. P. E. Bach's *Essay* is also apparent in the *Instructions on the Art of Playing the Piano Forte or Harpsichord* issued a year after Türk's work by Jan Dussek, the famous Czech pianist and composer, who was himself a former student of C. P. E. Bach. Similarly Muzio Clementi, often mentioned as the first musician whose entire activity—as performer, composer, pedagogue, publisher, and manufacturer—was focused on the piano and who provided an influential link to the Romantic age of piano music with his *Introduction to the Art of Playing on the Piano Forte* (1801), gave credit to C. P. E. Bach's *Versuch* as a basis of his knowledge: "Whatever I know about fingering and the new style, in short, whatever I understand of the pianoforte, I have learned from this book."[34]

＊

It is curious that the development of keyboard technique was linked to an instrument that, though capable of the most expressive means, was destined to remain limited to use in the home. Yet, in this particular role it was also eventually superseded by the piano. In the largest sense, the fortepiano's name covers the instrument's brilliance on the stage as well as its intimacy in a small room. The instrument served in a wide range of *Hausmusik*, from amateur performance on a widened social scale to virtuoso study of unequaled splendor, from four-hand versions of chamber music and orchestral literature to the totally novel solo repertoire of the Romantic age, and the gamut of these functions was foreshadowed in Mozart's work.

3

The Last Years of Travel

✳

During the years of the Italian sojourn, 1769–73, Mozart wrote no keyboard compositions. He was principally involved with opera and other dramatic works both in Italy and during intermittent returns to Salzburg. From this period come the operas *Mitridate, rè di Ponto* (1770) and *Lucio Silla* (1772), Mozart's first essays in opera seria; the musical play *Ascanio in Alba* (1771); the oratorio *La Betulia liberata* (1771); and the serenata *Il sogno di Scipione* (1772), the latter commissioned for, and presumably presented during, the festivities surrounding the installation of the new archbishop Hieronymus von Colloredo at Salzburg in 1772. Even the motet *Exsultate, jubilate* K. 165 (1773) demonstrates in its patently operatic expression the pervasiveness of the Italian vocal art.

But he also composed close to twenty symphonies. Their number and variety manifest a stylistic development that was tied in a special way to the circumstances of composition. As we know, Mozart visited Italy three times, there encountering the new symphonic style that had evolved from the form of the Italian opera overture. Through his early association with J. C. Bach, Mozart had already absorbed, indirectly but thoroughly, many of the elements of instrumental style associated with the opera buffa, as is evident in the eight-year-old's first symphonies, K. 16 and K. 19.[1]

In 1767, however, when the family traveled to Vienna (where they remained for over a year), he was to meet a somewhat different school of symphonic writing, that of the Austrians as represented by the works of Wagenseil and Holzbauer and by the early symphonies of Haydn. The influence proved to be immediately decisive: Mozart embraced the formal organization of the four-movement cycle and displayed divergent but characteristic Viennese traits, which included touches of baroque affinity (e.g., a juxtaposition of contrasting orchestral forces and a pronounced use of contrapuntal technique; see K. Anh. 221/45a) and a more progressive handling of first-movement form (see K. 48).[2] The influence of Haydn is again seen in works from the early 1770s and particularly suggested in the Symphony in D Major K. 133.[3] Indeed, the symphonies written during this period demonstrate a certain vacillation resulting from the nature of the circumstances: Mozart wrote symphonies while in Italy but also in Salzburg, always composing with characteristic sensitivity to the prevailing style and his particular audience. It was from the Italian symphony that he derived the form that was to become a norm for his clavier sonatas.

While on the first Italian trip at Lodi, Mozart composed his first string quartet K. 80 (73f)—the inception of his involvement with a genre that was to prove of singular importance in his work. His models were again Italian, in particular suggesting the style of Giambattista Sammartini (1770–75). Yet the *galant* symphonic quality of the first quartet (1770) and of the set of three string divertimentos K. 136–138 (125a–c) was soon superseded by part-writing of genuine chamber music, a true quartet style, in the group of six quartets K. 155–160 (134a, 134b, 157–159, 159a), most of which were written in Milan in 1772–73. Nonetheless, as Alfred Einstein pointed out, even in the first quartet one sees evidence of a contrapuntal expression, "a turn to the 'learned.' "[4] This tendency is considerably more pronounced in the six Viennese string quartets K. 168–173 written in 1773, whose fugal finales represent a kind of tour de force reminiscent of the similar finales in Haydn's Op. 20. It is worth noting that the same tendency emerges in the finale of Mozart's Piano Concerto in D Major K. 175, a work that stands isolated as the first totally original concerto after the concerto arrangements made in 1767 and 1772.

WORKS OF EARLY MATURITY: VIENNA, SALZBURG, AND MUNICH

During the summer of 1773, Mozart, accompanied by his father, went to Vienna presumably with the hope of securing a position. The Mozarts returned to Salzburg in September, and among the works Mozart completed were the String Quintet in B-flat Major K. 174 (begun in early 1773, the quintet—Mozart's first—was revised in December of that year) and the Piano Concerto in D Major K. 175. In both works, Mozart eventually rejected the original last movement (and in K. 174, the trio of the minuet). The new finale of the quintet, a movement of large proportions, exhibits remarkably fine part-writing. Conversely, in the concerto Mozart ultimately decided to abandon the idea of a contrapuntal finale, substituting a set of variations (the so-called Rondo in D Major K. 382, composed in 1782, which he used for performances in Vienna).

The main theme of the original finale is introduced by the orchestra in strict canon. The piano takes up the theme in a singular manner, rendering it in a decorated form of rococo elegance yet maintaining strict imitation while the orchestra restates the unadorned form of the canon. A brilliance of sonority results, in part owing to the choice of key and a scoring that includes trumpets; it is reflected in a keyboard texture, new in Mozart's work, whose virtuosity balances the orchestral forces throughout.

The finale provides, as do the other movements, a summary of pianistic idiom. Alberti and Murky basses are employed in characteristic manner. Alberti basses accompany the presentation of themes of varied character; they serve equally as support suggesting an orchestral tutti (for the first movement's principal theme) or as accompaniment to the most expressive melody (see also page 59). By contrast, because of the technical complexity of the pattern, especially in fast tempos, the Murky bass appears mostly at cadences. Passage work consisting of scales and arpeggios, or their combination, is written largely for the right hand; in its variety and difficulty it displays an imagination and style distinctly surpassing the writing of any contemporary. Moreover, arpeggios assume a certain focus; they appear most often either in sequential repetitions or in intricately broken patterns.

In general, the keyboard writing is oriented toward a pianistic expression of orchestral material and idiom. A motif from the exposition of the first movement that seems so totally characteristic of an orchestral *buffo* style is directly transferred from the orchestral score to the keyboard part (3.1). While this is not unusual in concertos of the time, certain episodes, for example, the figuration of the right hand coupled with crossing over of the left hand in the finale, point to a rather different assimilation of the symphonic idiom. Dramatic contrast and development are entrusted to the piano, a procedure that places the concerto partners in greatest relief.

Conversely, the Andante, ma un poco adagio exhibits a lyricism that is achieved by decidedly pianistic expressions (3.2). The cantabile character gains in contrast through the variety of accompaniments of the left hand, through shifts in register involving both hands, as well as through dynamics, stressed in the orchestral accompaniment.

*

Two keyboard compositions—the set of Six Variations in G Major K. 180 (173c) on the aria "Mio caro Adone" from the opera *La fiera di Venezia* by Antonio Salieri and the set of Twelve Variations in C Major K. 179 (189a) on a minuet by the composer and oboist Johann Christian Fischer—form a chronological frame for the Piano Concerto in D Major K. 175. Both works

3.1. Concerto in D Major K. 175, 1st movement, mm. 67–71

3.2. Concerto in D Major K. 175, 2d movement, mm. 23–29

assume a special position in Mozart's stylistic development, though they represent rather different approaches to the variation form.

In number, scale, and manner, the Six Variations K. 180 (173c) are in the tradition of the variations written in the Netherlands during the winter of 1766. These variations emphasize melodic elaboration given largely to the right hand, as did the variations on Dutch songs K. 24 and K. 25. Unlike the earlier sets, however, they no longer contain the types of rhythmic variation (e.g., diminution) prompted by the character of the harpsichord. Rather, they gain an expressive quality by use of *forte*, *piano*, and *sforzando*. The sonority is enhanced by writing for the left hand that includes octaves, chords, and figures of special melodic interest, as well as accompanying patterns marked by arpeggios or the Alberti bass. Evident is an integrity of part-writing that also becomes clear through the writing for the left hand, where motifs complement the general patterns of variation appearing in the right hand. The vocal quality of the theme is sustained throughout the set by the general cantilena in the right hand, the figurations of which are enhanced through the use, for the first time in Mozart's variation form, of varied phrasings and articulations. With regard to structure, one sees an increasing differentiation; also for the first time, the set closes with a variation that stands in contrast, both in meter and character, to the others. Through its pairing with the penultimate variation, an Adagio, a distinct form begins to emerge. The final variation gains in brilliance by an increased tempo and by other expressions of virtuosity, in K. 180 (173c) particularly evident in the last measures of rolled chords.

The Twelve Variations K. 179 (189a) demonstrate in basic outline the form that was to remain typical in later sets of piano variations. A heightened sense of structure is suggested through the keyboard writing: a series of variations clearly culminates in the tenth, characterized by octave passages involving both hands, and this is followed by an Adagio variation that leads into the final Allegro variation. Melodic transformation assumes new importance in these variations, as is apparent in the Adagio, whose florid treatment of the theme includes the use of broken octaves in addition to the principal means of scale elaboration (3.3). The final Allegro makes use of a figure that contributes to the work's flamboyant character in a unique manner. The accompaniment in the first part of the variation consists of an arpeggio pattern. In the second part, this pattern is, at first, transferred to the right hand (which nonetheless maintains the melodic outline); the passage gains in brilliance and sonority as the left hand joins in the arpeggios. While the transfer of patterns has become a feature, it is usually initiated in the right hand; here, however, the reverse procedure raises the level of virtuosity and gives to the concluding variation the character of an étude. Indeed, this set presents a number of novel keyboard

*3.3. Variations on a Minuet of J. C. Fischer K. 179 (189a), variation 11,
mm. 42–50*

idioms. The second and fourth variations show a transfer of motifs: in the
second, this appears as melodically imitative texture, while in the fourth, a
typical right hand tremolo pattern finds expression in the left hand. The increasing role assumed by the left hand is demonstrated in the fifth variation.
In the ninth variation, a polyphonic texture is suggested through the crossing
of hands, but it is the right hand (and not, as usually, the left) that alternates
between registers, while the left hand maintains the harmonic support in an
inner voice (3.4). The keyboard writing in this set suggests a type of work in
which bravura both in invention and texture was the aim, and as we know,
Mozart performed these variations frequently and with success as he established himself as a pianist.[5] Relevant in this connection are the observations of
Michael Kelly, the singer who first performed the role of Figaro, who commented in particular on Mozart's improvisational talents and in that context
on the strength of Mozart's left hand.[6]

✳

Mozart's first extant solo keyboard sonatas K. 279–283 (189d–h) and K.
284 (205b) date from early 1775; they were apparently composed in Munich.[7]
Mozart was there to oversee the production of *La finta giardiniera*, the comic
opera for which he had obtained a commission the previous summer. But he

3.4. Variations on a Minuet of J. C. Fischer K. 179 (189a), variation 9, mm. 1–8

took an active part also in other phases of Munich's cultural life; indeed, the essential impetus for the composition of these sonatas seems to have been their anticipated performance. Evidently, Mozart intended the six sonatas to form a series, as is suggested by the key scheme that outlines the "flat side" of the circle of fifths with the first four sonatas and the "sharp side" with the last two. Though only the last sonata was published—and not until 1782—these works were widely disseminated. Mozart performed them frequently and to great effect (he described them as "my difficult sonatas")[8] while at Munich and later in 1777 and 1778 at Augsburg and Mannheim.

The sonatas of 1775 represent the first collection of the mature young artist (in 1766 Mozart had composed four solo sonatas K. Anh. 199–202 [33d–g], but these have been lost), and they demonstrate a new depth of musical thought, which finds expression in a comparable advance in keyboard writing. Their particular change in style may have been due to the influence of Haydn, whose symphonies and quartets had already impressed Mozart as he approached these genres. During the middle and late 1760s and early 1770s, Haydn's work with the keyboard sonata reveals a significant evolution from the divertimento style.[9] The classical sonata now begins to assume a stature comparable to that of the symphony and quartet. Indicative is the powerful Sonata in C Minor (H. XVI:20) composed in 1771—one of a group stemming from the period 1765–71 and a work notable for fluid, expansive structures exhibiting a rather improvisatory quality—and the set of six sonatas (H. XVI: 21–26) composed in 1773 and published in February 1774 at Vienna as Op. 13.

This collection of six sonatas was dedicated to Haydn's patron, Prince Nikolaus Esterházy, and represents the first publication of Haydn's sonatas intended for a larger public—previous works had been circulated in individual manuscript copies or prints.[10] Compared to the earlier works, these sonatas appear more conservative in manner and approach, partly because of the intended dedicatee and partly because of their presumed audience among *Kenner und Liebhaber*, but they demonstrate certain stylistic features: a particularly expressive use of minor keys for secondary themes in first movements (all of which are in sonata form), the casting of three of the second movements in the minor mode, and the use of variation form in two finale movements, a choice that Mozart doubtless found attractive. Mozart probably became acquainted with these works while in Salzburg. Like Mozart, Michael Haydn, Joseph's younger brother, was in 1774 (the publication date of the Esterházy Sonatas) in service at the Salzburg archiepiscopal court and probably would have received a copy of his brother's published work.

We can trace to Haydn certain procedures of composition in Mozart's works, above all motivic development. But of equal interest are new expressions of pianistic idiom that also apparently stem from Mozart's acquaintance with Haydn's music. Most notable is the inclusion of passage work (scales or arpeggios) that is shared between the hands and produces a continuous line.[11] The writing usually covers a wide range of the keyboard and favors a colorful exchange of registers. But whereas Haydn uses such figures in rather free distribution between right and left hands, Mozart's writing suggests a more strictly polyphonic texture. Indeed, passages that combine the two hands in octaves, a characteristic feature of Haydn's keyboard style, are largely absent from Mozart's work. Also reminiscent of Haydn's style is the use of the harmonic "pedal," a keyboard expression of the symphonic style (3.5). Mozart's varied use of these idioms invariably exhibits the more natural disposition toward the piano.

A new attention to the expressive possibilities of the piano is evident throughout these sonatas in an unprecedented number of dynamic markings. While dynamic indications were employed in the variation sets, K. 180 (173c) and K. 179 (189a), they assume a much more prominent role in these sonatas.

3.5. Sonata in F Major K. 280 (189e), 3d movement, mm. 142–48

In addition to *piano, forte,* and *fp*, more highly differentiated markings are seen: *pianissimo, crescendo,* and *decrescendo*. A focused juxtaposition of dynamics becomes a feature of these sonatas, intensifying dramatic contrast by the association of certain dynamics with particular registers.

Similarly, phrase markings, both in their increased use and differentiation, demonstrate an advance over those in the concerto and the variation sets: they provide a more detailed notation of pianistic touch. A wide variety of articulation is indicated through the use of the staccato dot, wedge, and slur. It is clear that Mozart was beginning to distinguish between the two related forms of the staccato marking and that the wedge often represented a sharper articulation closer to that of an accent. Eva and Paul Badura-Skoda have rightly pointed out that, considering Mozart's varied use of these articulation signs throughout his manuscripts, it is not appropriate, nor perhaps even possible, to assign categorically the function of the wedge and staccato on a "purely philological basis."[12] Nonetheless, it is evident that here begins a process of differentiation that was to evolve in Mozart's work with demonstrably specific meaning, especially in the later solo sonatas and *Klavierstücke*.[13] In this first collection of mature sonatas, it also becomes evident that the use of slurs results from a new effort to achieve a greater expressiveness.[14] They appear, for example, in *cantabile* phrasing no longer primarily assigned to the right hand. Such phrasing also begins to define inner voices, thus contributing to the integrity of the part-writing.

Another type of articulation, the *appoggiato* (often referred to as a keyboard *portamento*), indicated by a slur connecting several notes marked with staccato dots, gains in significance throughout these sonatas (3.6). Particular care in specifying varieties of articulation and dynamic accents is also suggested in such passages as the one in 3.7. Similarly meticulous seems the application of trills and appoggiaturas. The overall result is a special brilliance, a bravura quality that pervades these sonatas.

The greatest display of virtuosity appears in final movements and may have

3.6. Sonata in D Major K. 284 (205b), 3d movement, mm. 9–17

3.7. Sonata in B-flat Major K. 281 (189f), 3d movement, mm. 52–59

been prompted by the wish to balance the more expanded forms of the first and second movements. The finale of the Sonata in B-flat Major K. 281, for example, is characteristic of a type of rondo that often recurs in Mozart's later works. The return of one of the episodes suggests a rondo pattern approaching sonata form, yet the reappearance of the original theme at a point corresponding to the sonata recapitulation shows in this case a transformation to an almost improvisational style.

The Sonata in D Major K. 284 stands apart from the others in the series. This work was composed later and represents, in its size and scope, an altogether different style, one that may have been prompted by the circumstances of its composition. The sonata was the result of a commission from the Baron Thaddäus von Dürnitz, a Munich musical amateur. The first movement in particular exhibits a patently orchestral idiom; though fully adapted to pianistic realization, it strongly suggests a keyboard arrangement of a symphonic score. Such a strong emphasis upon the symphonic idiom is new in Mozart's pianistic style. Writing for the two hands in octaves is now introduced with particular emphasis; a leaning towards the orchestral style is also stressed through the featured use of pedal points. Patterns combining tremolo with a harmonic outline in the bass are especially suggestive of orchestral figuration (3.8).

That Mozart singled this work out as a "concert sonata" is evident from its breadth as much as from its stylistic novelties. Of special interest is the middle movement, an Andante entitled *Rondeau en Polonaise*, whose theme is varied upon every successive appearance. The movement shows an intimacy of character that seems to foreshadow the later character piece for piano; as the rondo melody appears for the last time, this quality is enhanced by the treatment of the melodic line in octaves distributed over both hands (3.9; for a discussion of the last movement, see pages 49–50).

MANNHEIM AND PARIS SONATAS

Mozart returned from Munich to Salzburg in March 1775. He did not compose any new sonatas for the piano until October and November 1777, on his journey to Mannheim. During the fall of 1777, Mozart, accompanied by his mother, set out on a tour of principal cities in southern Germany in the hope of securing a court appointment. The first stop was Munich, but no opportunities seemed to be available at the Electoral court. From there, Mozart proceeded to Augsburg, Leopold's native town, where he met Johann Andreas Stein and became acquainted with the instruments the latter had built. As we know from several letters, Mozart continued to perform the six sonatas

3.8. Sonata in D Major K. 284 (205b), 1st movement, mm. 14–16

3.9. Sonata in D Major K. 284 (205b), 2d movement, mm. 27–36

composed during his earlier stay at Munich. As is also clear from the letters, however, he did improvise several keyboard works. Indeed, improvisation may have been a basis for the Sonata in C Major K. 309, one of two sonatas written subsequently in Mannheim, where the Mozarts arrived on 30 October after the stopover at Augsburg en route.

The C Major Sonata K. 309 (284b) and a second work written in Mannheim, the Sonata in D Major K. 311 (284c), contain pianistic idioms that reflect to a certain degree the influence of the orchestral style and expression so characteristic of the composers active in Mannheim at this time. A new attention to the coloristic possibilities of the piano emerges. Passage work extends as a matter of course throughout the range of the keyboard, and thematic material is freely distributed over different registers. (It should be noted that the differences among registers were especially pronounced in timbres of the eighteenth-century instrument.) An explicit orchestral style (not unlike that of the *Dürnitz* Sonata) is evident, especially in passages written in octaves for both hands (as in the opening of K. 309). Passages suggestive of string figurations abound. An accompanimental figure, best described as an oscillating bass, enters into prominence. This familiar pattern, involving two notes of the harmony, provides a particularly clear and light texture (3.10).

The Mannheim style was, in general, predicated on dynamic contrast and

3.10. Sonata in C Major K. 309 (284b), 1st movement, mm. 8–14

effect. Certain other characteristics, however, are associated with its expression. Instances of the Mannheim "rocket" and dramatic echo occur in Mozart's sonatas but do not assume exaggerated significance. Both the "rocket"—an ascending figure based upon a scale or triad—and echo repetitions, often in different registers, appear in the Sonata in C Major K. 309. As has been observed, these melodic features, though generally linked to the Mannheim style, were actually characteristic of Italian orchestral and dramatic music.[15] Nonetheless, they maintained a special association with Mannheim, enough so for Mozart's sister to comment after receiving a copy of the Sonata in C Major that "anyone could see it was composed in Mannheim" and for Leopold Mozart to remark in a letter to his son that "it has something of the mannered Mannheim style about it, but so little that your own good style is not spoilt."[16]

Dynamic contrasts figure more prominently throughout these two sonatas; they are especially noticeable in the second movement, which was written— as the following letter from Mozart to his father suggests—in the manner of a character study of Rosa Cannabich, eldest daughter of the violinist Christian Cannabich, leader of the Mannheim orchestra.

> I had already finished the Allegro, as you know, on the day after my arrival, and thus had only seen Mlle. Cannabich once. Young Danner [the son of Christian Danner, a Mannheim violinist] asked me how I thought of composing the Andante. I said that I would make it fit closely the character of Mlle. Rosa. When I played it, it was an extraordinary success. Young Danner told me so afterwards. It really is a fact. She is exactly like the Andante.[17]

This movement abounds with detailed expressive indications to which Mozart himself referred. "The Andante will give us the most trouble, for it is full of expression and must be played accurately and with exact shades of forte and piano, precisely as they are marked."[18] Not only do dynamics and differentiation of touch now influence the writing, but they lead to a variety of textures, demonstrably contrapuntal at times, which are in themselves variously combined. The emphasis on the registers of the piano continues to be a feature but gains in effect through their frequent juxtaposition, and in fact, the movement concludes with a cadence in a strikingly low register.

A new use of measured tremolo appears in the concluding movement of the C Major Sonata, which again appears to show traces of Mannheim orchestral sonority. At the same time, Mozart's ever-growing acquaintance with a variety of particular instruments seems to have decisively influenced his approach to writing for the piano, as can be gathered from the following letter written by Mozart's mother to his father and dated 28 December 1777.

> Everyone thinks the world of Wolfgang, but indeed he plays quite differently from what he used to in Salzburg—for there are pianofortes here in Mannheim, on which he plays so extraordinarily well that people say they have never heard the like. In short everyone who has heard him says that he has not got his equal. Although Beecke has been performing here and Schubart too, yet everyone says that Wolfgang surpasses them in beauty of tone, quality and execution.[19]

But Mannheim offered no more substantial career opportunities to Mozart than had Munich. And at Leopold's forceful prompting, Mozart finally left, having spent more than four months there, and headed for Paris. In Mozart's search for a position or even for major commissions, Paris was also to prove disappointing. As Baron von Grimm wrote Leopold, the city was too preoccupied with the controversy over operatic styles as represented by Gluck and Piccini to take notice of Wolfgang.[20] Indeed, aside from some symphonies for the *Concert spirituel*,[21] only a few compositions actually date from the months in Paris and among these there is only one sonata for piano, the one in A Minor K. 310 (300d).

The first piano sonata in a minor key (there were to be only two), is marked by a grave mood, and its intensity results in writing that suggests a different conception of piano composition. Mozart adapts an (essentially abstract) orchestral sonority to the piano and combines it with sonorities wholly pianistic. The apparent emphasis is on the realization of a full orchestral sound and not simply on the transference of a certain orchestral character. We may be dealing with impressions Mozart gained from the sound of the large orchestras at Mannheim and Paris.

In addition to a thickened texture, the sonata's opening chordal pattern in the left hand suggests a subtlety of part-writing that develops through the series of retardations and resolutions following the first four measures (3.11).

3.11. Sonata in A Minor K. 310 (300d), 1st movement, mm. 1–7

3.12. Sonata in A Minor K. 310 (300d), 2d movement, mm. 81–86

Indeed, an increasingly pronounced polyphonic texture, a general feature of this sonata, assumes special prominence in the first movement's development. Prominence is also given to particular rhythmic motifs, both in the first and third movements, and this leads to passages stressing various registers but most notably to statements of melodic material in the bass register. Another notable aspect of the work is keyboard writing that extends over the entire range of the piano, producing a strong concentration on color as well as sonority (3.12).

The intensity and scope of musical ideas necessitate commensurately larger dimensions of structure. In the development section of the second movement a striking and extended passage, fantasia-like in nature, introduces in the bass register an arpeggiated triplet figuration that is subsequently transformed into a polyphonic texture in the treble through a series of suspensions. This represents a wholly new approach, seemingly prompted by greater demands for piano sound.

A comparison has been drawn with the keyboard style of Johann Schobert (ca. 1735–67) whose brilliant and passionate expression apparently remained influential in Paris even after his untimely death.[22] Mozart had arranged movements of a Schobert sonata in his earliest concerto endeavors, and evidently, he remained sufficiently interested in Schobert's keyboard music to recommend it to his pupils in Paris during his sojourn in 1778.[23] Similarities between Mozart's Sonata in A Minor and a sonata by Schobert (Op. 17, No. 1, first movement) have been pointed out.[24] The suggestion of a direct influence gains in strength in view of certain stylistic features of Schobert's music. The use of sequences in the development of material, for example, seems especially characteristic of Schobert's writing, and Mozart's use of the same device forms a noteworthy analogy.

✳

Eight sonatas for violin and piano written during the same period represent a second phase of Mozart's involvement with the genre. In contrast to the earlier accompanied sonatas, written in Paris, London, and The Hague, these works are true ensemble sonatas, and the pianistic writing mirrors a significant change. Here, in fact, is the inception of a chamber music style that attains major importance in later periods of Mozart's pianistic work.

A strong influence toward this new approach seems to have been the music of Joseph Schuster (1748–1812); Kapellmeister at the Dresden court, with whose music Mozart became familiar while at Munich during the fall of 1777. Mozart wrote to his father: "I send my sister herewith six duets for clavicembalo and violin by Schuster, which I have often played here. They are not bad. If I stay on I shall write six myself in the same style, as they are very popular here. My main object in sending them to you is that you may amuse yourself à deux".[25] Mozart was, indeed, to write a set of six sonatas, which he later published as his Op. 1 in 1778. Four of the works in this set, the Sonatas K. 301 (293a) in G Major, K. 302 (293b) in E-flat Major, K. 303 (293c) in C Major, and K. 305 (293d) in A Major, were written in Mannheim in early 1778, while the remaining two, the Sonatas K. 304 (300c) in E Minor and K. 306 (300l) in D Major, were composed in Paris during the summer of that year. Engraved in Paris in 1778 by the publisher Sieber, they were dedicated to Maria Elisabeth, the wife of the Elector of the Palatinate, and they are often referred to as the Palatinate or Mannheim sonatas. The Sonata in C Major

K. 296, written for Mlle. Therese-Pierron Serrarius, a pupil of Mozart's in Mannheim, also dates from this sojourn. Together with the Sonata in B-flat Major K. 378 (317d) composed either in Salzburg in 1779 or later in Vienna in 1781 and four sonatas written in Vienna in the spring and summer of 1781, it was incorporated into Mozart's Op. 2.

In a letter dated 14 February 1778, Mozart refers to his sonatas composed in Mannheim as duets for clavier and violin,[26] and this suggests the different conception inherent in these works: now the violin assumes a role equal to that of the piano. Einstein has referred to these compositions as Mozart's "first really *concertante* sonatas";[27] and it is clear that a chief feature is the exchange of material, both melodic and accompanimental, between instruments. Though the violin part maintains its doubling role to some extent, it is distinctly different from that of the childhood works. It serves an intensely expressive purpose, not only enriching the texture but stating, jointly with the piano, principal musical ideas.

The resulting change in the relationship of the two instruments affects the pianistic texture. Compared with the solo piano works, it is decidedly thinner throughout, a change obviously prompted by the new role of the violin. Indeed, many of the accompanimental figures that would contribute to a full keyboard texture are now assumed by the violin. A single bass line often results, and there are rarely more than two simultaneously sounded tones in the part of each hand. A typical piano accompaniment is the combination of sparse bass in the left hand and broken chord patterns in the right hand. Supporting the thematic material in the violin part (thematic material subsequently exchanged between the two instruments), the keyboard figuration takes on virtuoso quality in the new accompanimental assignments for the right hand.

The Rondeau, Andante grazioso of the Sonata in E-flat Major K. 302 contains a striking example of a broken chord figure shared between hands in intertwined position. Türk refers to this pattern as *Eindringen der Hände*.[28] It is a sophistication in Mozart's cross-hand technique, especially by virtue of its placement in a high register (3.13). Conversely, a novel touch in exploiting a low register appears in the Tempo di Menuetto of the Sonata in C Major K. 303, where an accompanimental figure (first stated by the violin) is shifted to the bass with singular emphasis through a trill, the employment of which in the lowest register is rare.

References to Mannheim influences gain explicit illustration in the first movements of the Sonatas in E-flat K. 302 and A Major K. 305. The so-called Mannheim crescendo, a pattern absent from Mozart's solo sonatas of the period, is cultivated and used to advantage in a texture augmented by the violin part. The E-flat Major Sonata begins with a typically symphonic *forte* state-

3.13. Sonata in E-flat Major K. 302 (293b) for piano and violin, 2d movement, mm. 112–17

ment in both instruments leading in octaves from tonic to dominant and answered by a lyrical phrase that returns to the tonic, to the opening motif in octaves, and to the *forte* sonority. The characteristic answer, however, is this time extended into a rising melodic line that grows, by exchange between the two instruments, over two octaves, whereas in the A Major Sonata a corresponding passage largely results through steadily thickening textures of the piano part expanding in registers.

The use of octaves as an essential element of the musical texture marks the highly expressive Sonata in E Minor K. 304, an unusual key for Mozart. The sonata may be said to occupy a singular position in Mozart's chamber music, attaining a depth of emotional expression that places it on a par with the Sonata in A Minor for piano, written during the same period. A rich sonority distinct from the generally thin texture of the piano scoring in these sonatas is evident, partly through the very presence of the violin and partly through writing that, especially in the sonata's first movement, leads to an ensemble of remarkable invention. Octave passages are written for both the right and left hands, as well as for the violin part, and these involve essential thematic material. In the second movement, Tempo di menuetto, the E major episode exhibits a type of chordal writing that elicits the strongest contrast of mood. Uncommon in Mozart's work, it forms a passage whose sound and requisite pianistic touch are veritably Schubertian (3.14; one is reminded of Schubert's Sonatina in D

3.14. Sonata in E Minor K. 304 (300c) for piano and violin, 2nd movement, mm. 94–103

Major, Op. 137, No. 1). An expansion of technique is suggested in passages involving trills; in association with the ornamentation in the violin part, trills are eventually added simultaneously in both hands. The use of ornaments in both hands was noted in the Piano Sonata in A Minor, and its presence here, as there, documents a subtly absorbed virtuoso quality.

With one exception, the six Palatinate sonatas consist of two movements, suggesting the influence of J. C. Bach, who favored this scheme. The first three-movement work, the Sonata in C Major K. 296, stands apart from the Palatinate group. Mozart added this sonata of 1778 to the collection published in 1781 in Vienna as his Op. 2, a collection known as the Auernhammer sonatas.[29] The last sonata in the Palatinate series, the Sonata in D Major K. 306, demonstrates in its three movements expansive structures and brilliant pianistic writing that reflect the work's generally grand nature (with regard to scope, a parallel may be drawn with the solo Piano Sonata K. 284 in the same key, the *Dürnitz* Sonata).

In the first movement, a particular pianistic style influences the handling of musical ideas. For example, the spirit of development is produced by an extensive series of arpeggios that are shared between the hands. The brilliance of this treatment is consistent with the general tone of the composition and its characteristically grand gestures. Of the three movements, the last features the most obvious virtuoso writing. It presents an interesting formal structure comparable to that of the first movement of the Sonata in C Major K. 303, where an initial Adagio recurs between Allegro sections. (A sonata by Schuster has been cited as the model for K. 303.)[30] In the finale of K. 306 the sections Allegretto and Allegro offer contrast in meter as well as in tempo. In addition, the second Allegro culminates in a *cadenza in tempo* marked Allegro assai for both instruments. Nonetheless, the focus remains on the piano part, which displays a summary of bravura techniques and exploits the full range of the instrument's expressive powers. K. 306 occupies a special position; beyond maintaining the balance between violin and piano parts, the writing now more strongly represents the *concertante* style.

LATER MUNICH WORKS

Mozart left Paris in early fall 1778 to accept the position of *Konzertmeister* in Salzburg, a position in which he functioned also as court organist. Evidently not anxious to return, Mozart traveled to Mannheim and Munich before eventually arriving in Salzburg in January 1779. He was to remain in Salzburg for almost two years, during which he was chiefly involved with duties at the archiepiscopal court. There he composed a variety of instrumental music, the Sinfonia Concertante for violin and viola being the most notable, but apparently no solo piano works. In the summer of 1780 Mozart again received a commission to write an opera for performance during carnival at Munich. The work was *Idomeneo*, and it was apparently during Mozart's stay in Munich in the late fall and winter of 1780–81 that the next three solo sonatas for piano were composed. These compositions were long considered products of the Paris sojourn in 1778, but recent investigations, particularly those of Wolfgang Plath, have shown that they derive from a later period.[31]

The Sonatas in C Major K. 330 (300h), A Major K. 331 (300i), and F Major K. 332 (300k) offer a summary of keyboard idioms as well as novel expressions of pianistic writing. Certain stylistic features are again suggestive of the Mannheim influence, most strongly in the Sonata in C Major. Repetition of particular motifs combined with dynamic contrasts, certain bass patterns, octave passages shared between the left and right hands, and the extensive use of tremolo are all stylistic traits associated with Mozart's Mannheim sonatas.

On the other hand, the C Major Sonata's second movement, a highly expressive Andante cantabile, includes a striking pedal point effect in repeated sixteenth-note groups apparently meant to be played quasi-legato. As an accompanying pattern in a slow tempo and in the minor mode, it introduces an unusual piano sonority (3.15). Known as the *Trommelbass*, or drum bass, when it appears in moderate or quick tempo,[32] this typical keyboard idiom is here dramatically and thoroughly transformed. The movement is marked

3.15. Sonata in C Major K. 330 (300h), 2d movement, mm. 21–24

dolce, a term all-pervasive in later Mozart scores, which assists in defining both a pianistic touch and the general character of the movement. With this group of three sonatas and with the Sonata in A Minor K. 310, where the term *calando* had been used, a conspicuous differentiation of expressive directions appears.

The Sonata in A Major K. 331 (300i) is probably Mozart's most famous sonata. None of its movements is cast in sonata form; a set of variations forms the first movement, a minuet and trio the second, and the celebrated Rondo alla turca the third. Two of the variations in the first movement present familiar types of pianistic writing, but in notably different contexts. In the *minore*, the melody is repeated in octaves that, in the register of the right hand, contribute to the total sound a particular sonority deriving from a requisite *cantabile* touch. The technique of crossing of hands, firmly established in Mozart's work, meets with expanded treatment in the fourth variation. The crossing left hand presents the transformed theme in thirds, accompanied by "oscillating" chords in the right hand and bass support in the left.

The Rondo alla turca receives its characteristic janissary effects from the variety of keyboard writing suggestive of band instrumentations and also from colorful harmonic touches that feature the alternation between major and minor modes. The pervasive "drum" rhythm assumes a truly percussive sound through grace-note arpeggios. This noisy effect is heightened further in the coda, where appoggiaturas precede repeated chords in the right hand.

The Sonata in F Major K. 332 (300k) marks the greatest advance within these three works, both in its diversity of musical ideas and the resulting pianistic expressions. The first movement is characterized by a subtle yet rich harmonic language in sequences following the circle of fifths (a favored pattern of Mozart). This passage demonstrates a distinct pianistic pattern combining strong accents (especially through octaves in the left hand) with a syncopated *detaché* rhythm in the right hand. The sudden dynamic contrasts that stress the accents become more persistent and lead to cross-rhythms of great technical intricacy (3.16).

A comparison of the autograph with the first edition reveals interesting

3.16. Sonata in F Major K. 332 (300k), 1st movement, mm. 60–67

details in the history of the second movement (two versions are fully rendered in the *NMA*, though the variants apply only to the latter part of the movement).[33] Evidently, for the first edition Mozart had decided to richly embellish the recapitulation, and the resulting transformation featured increased sonorities as well as a certain type of coloratura writing for the piano. The rhapsodic elaboration of the melodic line, combined with augmented technical brilliance, imbues the recasting with a special emotional quality.

The third movement represents one of the largest and most varied last movements in all of Mozart's piano sonatas. Its brilliant passage work is underlined by a growing contrapuntal complexity that manifests itself in passages of concentrated and deft part-writing. This leads to the strongest contrast of textures (as well as of musical ideas) and contributes to the expansive structure of the movement. In contrast to the finale of the A Minor Sonata, K. 310 (300d), built essentially upon a single motive, this movement presents a veritable wealth of ideas.

VARIATIONS

Aside from the variations on an aria by Salieri K. 180 (173c), written in 1773, and those on the minuet by J. C. Fischer K. 179 (189c), composed in 1774, no independent sets of variations followed until 1778. Doubtless, Mozart continued to improvise series of variations, but evidently circumstances during the intervening years did not encourage their elaboration with a view toward publication. Only in Paris, where one of the most popular musical forms was that of the variation, did a distinct musical atmosphere prevail that led Mozart to compose two sets of variations in 1778. Both featured French tunes popular at the time: the Variations in E-flat Major K. 354 (299a) are based on the romance "Je suis Lindor" from Beaumarchais' *Le Barbier de Séville*, the music for which was presumably composed by Antoine Laurent Baudron (1724–1834), and the Variations in C Major K. 264 (315d) on the aria "Lison dormait" from the opéra comique *Julie* by Nicholas Dezède.[34] (The variations on "Je suis Lindor" were published, together with the sets on themes of Salieri and Fischer, by the French publisher Mme. Heina in Paris in 1778.)

Both Paris works follow the basic form established in the last movement of the *Dürnitz* Sonata, that is, a series marked by increasing technical brilliance into which are interpolated contrasts of texture, mode, tempo, and meter. But a cyclic sense of order is more strongly suggested in these sets through certain patterns or procedures of variation (sixteenth-note passage work, octaves, etc.) assigned in alternate sections to each hand; in the "Lindor" set, variations one and two, five and six, ten and eleven might serve as examples. The Adagio variation, as was also seen in the variation finale movement of the *Dürnitz* Sonata, is the one most richly ornamented. Yet the keyboard "coloratura" appears as an organic elaboration or transformation of the original theme, and while it is usually assigned to the right hand, the left hand assumes in the "Lison dormait" set, for the first time, a share of the varied theme.

The two sets of variations form a complementary pair, the "Lison dormait" variations being the more audaciously difficult of the two. In addition to a highly florid treatment of the theme in both hands, its Adagio variation features sustained trills for expressly dramatic purpose in passages that seem to have grown from the rhythmic complexity of the movement. The pianistic writing here dictates total independence of techniques in both hands. (In general, this set demonstrates a degree of difficulty that often characterizes Mozart's keyboard music in C major.) The final variation, an Allegro in contrasting triple meter, further heightens the bravura quality, culminating in a cadenza complete with a glissando in sixths and a scale in thirds for the right hand.

In this context, we must return, for more detailed consideration, to the two sets of variations that appear as movements of sonatas, both of them preceding the independent sets composed in Paris. The first is the finale movement of the 1775 Sonata in D Major (the *Dürnitz*) and the second is the last (second) movement of the Sonata in A Major K. 305 (293d) for piano and violin, composed in Mannheim in 1778. The finale of the *Dürnitz* Sonata consists of a set of twelve variations, the longest concluding movement in the series of solo sonatas composed in early 1775. The work's significance lies in the fact that it represents the first instance in which Mozart uses within a solo sonata the variation scheme that was to become the norm for his later sets and that here, also for the first time, Mozart interpolates a variation in the minor mode marked by highly expressive writing. In part, the latter seems to derive from a melody whose contours contain much chromaticism; a particularly full sonority of accompaniment appears again in the Sonata in A Minor K. 310 (300d), written three years later in Paris. The Adagio and Allegro, as final variations, contribute to formal balance.

A sense of structure is emphasized through pianistic features, many of which are to be repeated in Mozart's work in this genre. In addition to the major-minor contrast, there are other departures from typically varied series of melodic figuration. Variation nine is marked by an intricate contrapuntal fabric, and yet this relief from an intense virtuoso style leads to new concentrated pianistic interpretation of the theme in passages of paired octaves. As we have seen in other variation sets, florid elaboration marks the Adagio variation, but the pianistic brilliance, which first emerges in association with keyboard coloratura first in the *Dürnitz* Sonata, creates a momentum that now produces a change from sectional to continuous form. A freer handling of structure is also evident in the last variation. Here, thematic transformation derives partly from the change to triple meter, but genuine pianistic writing— broken octave patterns and *subito pianissimo* octaves—contributes to a sense of motivic development, providing a climactic conclusion for the variation movement and the sonata as a whole.

The characteristics observed in the sonatas for piano and violin composed in Mannheim and Paris in 1778, for example, the exchange of musical material between parts and the generally thinner piano scoring (serving to balance the emerging role of the violin), also manifest themselves in the variation movement of the Sonata in A Major K. 305 (293d). Yet greater freedom of texture now gives rise to a different chamber music style. Within the context of a variation for piano solo, deft duet writing is maintained, at the same time presenting pianistic scoring unusual for Mozart. Other passages of pianistic writing suggest, rather, an orchestral texture, which the violin part enhances with touches of color. An absorbingly delicate chamber music style is developed in passages where the exchange between players again and again influences the pianistic style (3.17).

IMPROVISATIONAL AND *CONCERTANTE* WORKS

The Prelude in C Major K. 284a, more familiarly known as the Capriccio in C Major K. 395 (300g), occupies a very special place in Mozart's keyboard oeuvre. Previously assigned to the year 1778, it actually derives (as is clear

*3.17. Sonata in A Major K. 305 (293d) for piano and violin, 2d
movement, variation 3, mm. 9–14*

from Wolfgang Plath's investigations) from an earlier period, the fall of 1777
and Mozart's sojourn in Munich.[35] Evidently, the Capriccio was the result of
a request by Mozart's sister Nannerl. In a letter dated, Salzburg, 29 September
1777, from Leopold Mozart to his son, Nannerl added a postscript to her
brother, then at Munich: "Please be so good as to send me a short preambu-
lum. But write one this time from C into B-flat, so that I may gradually learn
it by heart."[36] There followed on 11 October 1777, a letter from Mozart to his
father: "I enclose four preambula for her [Nannerl]. She will see and hear for
herself into what keys they lead."[37] The manuscript consists of four sections.
The first section or "prelude" modulates from C to B-flat; two shorter sections
follow in different keys, and the work is completed by an extended section in
C major marked capriccio. There is a similar case in which Mozart wrote a
prelude for Nannerl and announced it in a letter, dated Paris, 20 July 1778:

> Please forgive me for being so late in sending my congratulations. But I wanted to
> present my sister with a little Preambulum. The manner of playing it I leave to her
> own feeling. This is not the kind of prelude which passes from one key into another,
> but only a sort of Capriccio, with which to test a clavier. . . . You need not be very
> particular about the time. This is a peculiar type of piece. It is the kind of thing that
> may be played as you feel inclined.[38]

Plath has convincingly argued (*NMA* Serie IX/27/2) that the genesis of K.
284a must be understood in connection with Nannerl's postscript to the letter

of 29 September 1777 and not with Mozart's letter from the following year, as had been done in earlier interpretations. He pointed out that the "testing" described in Mozart's 1778 letter was one of the purposes of preludes in the contemporary musical practice of the time. Among the considerations involved were tuning, precision of attack, dynamic response, proper functioning of the key mechanism, and sonority of extreme registers.[39] But connected with the mechanical test of an instrument was the display of improvisatory skill that might link different keys. Improvisations, especially typical of eighteenth-century public performance, served to introduce the principal compositions of a program; they might be placed before, between, or after these works—as preludes, interludes, or postludes.[40] Thus this C Major Prelude represents a written-out improvisation of a type distinct from the variation sets or even cadenzas. While demonstrating the extraordinary imagination of Mozart, it remains thoroughly practical. Here one is offered a privileged glimpse into an art which by its very nature usually went unrecorded.

While the piece is written as a "sort of Capriccio, with which to test a clavier," it has a rather neutral quality—Mozart's personal musical expression is largely absent. Evident, however, is a keyboard writing that, while characteristically varied, presents an idiom unusual in Mozart's pianistic style. Certain keyboard figurations, as well as the almost explosive spontaneity of certain modulations, have prompted suggestions of possible influences from J. S. Bach and C. P. E. Bach. Hermann Abert's mention of a similarity to the keyboard style of both Bachs may have been prompted by such passages as that illustrated in 3.18.[41] Touches of conservative imitative texture may be observed at times, but they seem to be aimed at alternate hands rather than at alternate voices. Examination of the piano's mechanism and its expressive range may have given rise to passages marked Cantabile and Allegro assai. In the first, the chromatic writing offers a test of proper tuning, and in the second, an elaboration of pedal points provides a test of repeating efficiency of the key lever (3.19). The very free keyboard style runs the full range of the contemporary piano, from FF to f^3, and the piece as a whole is a display of bravura.

The Capriccio forms a link to what now assumes for the first time a certain measure of prominence in Mozart's pianistic writing: the concerto cadenza. The Concerto in D Major K. 175 of 1773, previously discussed, stands relatively isolated. Five further works of the genre followed later in the 1770s— the Concertos in B-flat Major K. 238, in F Major K. 242 (for three pianos), in C Major K. 246, in E-flat Major K. 271, and in E-flat Major K. 365 (316a, for two pianos)—and for all of them original cadenzas exist; yet the cadenzas are of distinctly different stature, commensurate with the different stature of the concertos themselves.

3.18. Prelude in C Major K. 284a, also known as Capriccio in C Major K. 395 (300g), mm. 7a–7e

It is worthwhile, in fact, to single out some characteristics of Mozart's concerto cadenzas of this period in order to gain a vantage point from which to view the varying importance of the works for which they were written, for the character of these works once again reflects the quality of Mozart's pianistic style. In the cadenzas for the first group of concertos, Mozart is already

3.19. Prelude in C Major K. 284a, also known as Capriccio in C Major K. 395 (300g), mm. 20–25

concerned with fusing consciously brilliant technique with motifs and ideas presented in the concerto itself. As more thematic material becomes integrated into the cadenzas, a greater variety of keyboard textures results, and while the cadenza begins to summarize and occasionally develop musical ideas, it offers new opportunity for solo display.

The most significant group of cadenzas belongs to the Concerto in E-flat Major K. 271, a work that occupies a unique position in Mozart's writing of the period, for it demonstrates an intensely dramatic relationship between soloist and orchestra. The cadenzas are now integrally connected with the concerto, and orchestral material is variously transformed in them, for instance, in figurations that reflect the orchestral climax preceding the first-movement cadenzas or in a contrapuntal passage that suggests the canonic beginning of the second movement.

The expressive quality of the Andantino is reflected in the cadenza for this movement with patterns that exploit the dark lower register (3.20). An alternate cadenza for the first movement contains a highly unusual passage that, enlarged in octaves, was to become a characteristic touch of nineteenth-century pianistic virtuosity (3.21), and the virtuoso quality of the last-movement cadenzas presents a considerable range of expression partly manifest through very specific tempo indications and dynamic markings. Nonetheless, Mozart gives even the most brilliant of these excursions motivic meaning, and he ties the cadenza inextricably to the rest of the movement. Such connection is even more pronounced in other cadenzas extant for this concerto. The beginning

3.20. Concerto in E-flat Major K. 271, cadenza to 2d movement, mm. 5–10

3.21. Concerto in E-flat Major K. 271, alternate cadenza to 1st movement, mm. 11–13

of a cadenza for the third movement consists of a veritable development of the principal theme.

More than two years had passed between the composition of the Concerto in D Major K. 175 and the three piano concertos written during the winter and spring of 1776 (in B-flat Major K. 238, in F Major K. 242, in C Major K. 246). The Concerto in D Major K. 175 represented Mozart's first totally original piano concerto, and its pianistic style emanated largely from the wish to establish a balance with the symphonic character of the orchestral accompaniment. Indeed, the presence of the orchestra is felt even in the solo statements of principal themes since they are often supported by an orchestral accompaniment that doubles the essential material. However, the concertos composed in 1776 are a decidedly different type of work in which a more distinct but subtle relationship exists between soloist and orchestra. This refinement can be traced to the experience Mozart had otherwise gained in dealing with the concerto genre. During 1775 Mozart had written a series of five violin concertos with himself as soloist in mind. These works are marked by a growing sensitivity towards the dramatic contrasts implicit in the concerto form, and they are also distinguished by a wealth of melodic invention.

The piano concertos that followed exhibit comparable variety and flexibility. The exposition of themes is, at times, now assumed by the piano, and the piano and orchestra often share in the presentation of musical ideas by exchange of motifs and phrases. At the same time, we can observe a new finesse in handling the pianistic medium, the result of Mozart's involvement with the forms of piano sonata and variation, and a greater sophistication of pianistic composition has now become part of Mozart's creative personality. Nonetheless, the greatest gain is the assured absorption of the *concertante* element. Against the background of the instrumental divertimento and serenade, a *concertante* quality had been deliberately cultivated in the Concertone in C Major K. 190 (186E) for two violins of 1774, and it also manifested itself in a special way in a pianistic genre: compositions for piano four-hands that are "the purest examples of the concertante style."[42] Two sonatas for piano four-hands from the early 1770s, the Sonatas in D Major K. 381 (K. 123a) and in B-flat Major K. 358 (K. 186c), call for an instrumental ensemble "intended for two partners of equal importance,"[43] and were written for performance by Mozart and his sister: "The first [Sonata in D major] . . . is best described as a reduction of an Italian symphony—a symphony in which individual groups of winds and strings, of tutti and soli are sharply distinguished. And the Andante contains a genuinely orchestral effect, the melody of the *primo* being doubled two octaves lower by the 'bassoon' or 'cello' of the *secondo*."[44]

The pianistic texture in these works found further expression in concertos for piano ensemble combining two and three pianos. The Concerto in F Major K. 242 for three pianos was composed in February 1776 and was written expressly for members of the Lodron family, a family of Salzburg nobility. This is an ingeniously designed composition, for its texture, suggesting an integrated ensemble, effectively belies what must have been a disparity among the original performers' talents (indeed, the third clavier poses fewer technical demands). Hence, the concerto lent itself to arrangement for two pianos, and Mozart made such a version about 1779, at a time when he was involved with the composition of ensemble concertos, including an original concerto for two pianos.

From the fall of 1777 until the fall of 1778, Mozart was in Mannheim and Paris and was influenced by the orchestral style then current and by the fashionable *sinfonia concertante*. While in Paris, Mozart composed the Concerto in C Major K. 299 (297c) for flute and harp—another dilettante concerto[45]—

and the much more significant (though not totally authenticated) Sinfonia Concertante in E-flat Major K. Anh. 9 (K. 297B or C14.01) for woodwinds.[46] Returning to Mannheim, he began in November 1778 a Double Concerto in D Major for piano and violin K. Anh. 56 (315f), and a Triple Concerto in A Major K. Anh. 104 (320e) for violin, viola, and cello was begun about a year later.[47] Neither was completed.

Two double concertos, however, were believed to have been completed in 1779[48] in Salzburg and these represent in effect companion works: the Sinfonia Concertante in E-flat Major K. 364 (320d) for violin and viola and the Concerto in E-flat Major K. 365 (316a) for two pianos. The Sinfonia Concertante stands as Mozart's highest achievement within the realm of the string concerto, and the Concerto for Two Pianos K. 365 (316a), evidently intended for performance by Mozart and his sister, is a work of comparable scale and texture. As in the Sinfonia Concertante (K. 364 [320d]), the Mannheim and Paris orchestral styles and their sonorities are reflected in the score and even in the brilliant writing in the solo parts. Particularly noteworthy are certain features of the orchestration that foreshadow the scope of later piano concertos: there are divided viola parts and Mozart later enriched the scoring for the first and third movements with clarinets, trumpets, and timpani for performances in 1781 and 1782 in Vienna.

It is interesting in this connection to recall the symphonic works discussed at the beginning of this chapter, for the earlier orchestral texture, the highly varied texture of the *concertante* works, and the developed pianistic style were all joined in a dramatic and unparalleled fashion in the Piano Concerto in E-flat Major K. 271, composed in 1777.

Mozart was asked to write the Concerto in E-flat Major K. 271 for Mlle. Jeunehomme, a French concert pianist who visited Salzburg while on tour during the winter of 1776–77. Mozart was always mindful of particular performers, yet the occasion of composing for this famous virtuoso pianist clearly prompted a special approach, possibly stemming from the wish to impress or challenge, or perhaps to recognize her extraordinary talent.[49] While relatively little is known about Mlle. Jeunehomme (although Mozart later encountered her again in Paris in 1778), his evident awareness of the soloist is made explicit in Mozart's inscription on the concerto, "written for Mlle. Jeunehomme."[50]

Towering above all of his previous essays in the genre, the Piano Concerto in E-flat Major K. 271, composed in January 1777, marks a crucial juncture in the development of Mozart's style. Like a bold announcement, the novel opening with its immediate juxtaposition of orchestra and soloist presents the challenge of concerto form in the symphonic age (3.22). The role of the piano

3.22. Concerto in E-flat Major K. 271, 1st movement, mm. 1–7

has become more assertive within a mature orchestral texture, and the structure results as much from the melding of forces as from their confrontation.

Especially interesting is the subtle pianistic outlining of this structure, as can be seen in the blending of soloistic trill and orchestral cadence before the solo exposition, an approach that foreshadows such transitions in Beethoven's later concertos. Similarly, the fabric of the concluding tutti is enhanced by reflective comment of the solo part, complete with trill and arpeggio. Throughout this work, Mozart heightens the contrast between the concerto partners by stressing changes in orchestral textures through the pianistic idiom; thus, his special use of the Alberti bass signals the launching of pointed virtuosity, as for example, in measure 69 of the first movement. Conversely, Mozart also employs the Alberti bass to introduce or distinguish an expressive melody, drawing attention to changes in pace or register.

The sophistication of the symphonic medium is expressed in an assured excellence of part-writing in the strings and analogous independence of woodwind parts. But in the second movement, the symphonic character gives way entirely to a chamber music texture. The immediate development of motivic material is echoed in the recapitulation, where dense canonic recollections of the opening tutti are shared by violins and piano after a dramatically introduced Neapolitan sixth: the real drama, here as elsewhere, lies in the ensemble of the concerto partners.

To a great extent, the coherence of the rondo arises once again through the contrast of forces. The solo statements of the rondo theme are complemented by the three cadenzas that anchor the form, and they in turn are inextricably woven into the theme's restatements and the episodes. A minuet with four variations figures as the most striking episode; in the course of these variations, the blending of pianistic and orchestral writing reaches a serene equilibrium that shows as much textural differentiation in one as it does in the other. The ornate solo cantilena meets with an accompaniment colored by the shades of *con sordino* and *senza sordino* and *pizzicato* and *col arco* until it rises to a point at which the most extensive transformation of the theme is marked by rhapsodic elaboration of the piano part.

✳

Figured bass parts exist for the Concertos in C Major K. 246 and E-flat Major K. 271, as they do for the Concerto in B-flat Major K. 238, the earliest of these three solo concertos, which are often considered as a group. But the particular circumstances of the C major and E-flat major compositions—the former composed for a dilettante, the Salzburg Countess Antonia Lützow, the latter for Mlle. Jeunehomme—led to accordingly different performance realizations. The one written out for the C Major Concerto is rich in detail and imaginative though modest, indicative of Mozart's consideration of the inexperienced soloist. The "realization" for the E-flat Concerto in the autograph, as well as in the solo part copied out by Nannerl and revised in details by Leopold,[51] presents a more flexible approach to the accompanying role of the solo instrument and results in the most highly varied keyboard part. In his edition of the work for the *NMA,* Christoph Wolff has pointed out textures of the solo part ranging from "akkordisch" and "Baßton oktaviert" to "ohne Baßlinie" and "pausierend."[52]

Eva and Paul Badura-Skoda have observed that "nowadays we no longer doubt that in performing his piano concertos Mozart used the piano as a continuo instrument."[53] Yet in the tradition of the time, the soloist also acted as conductor and was thus fully involved in the purely orchestral portions of the concerto. Whether supporting a given detail, enriching a thin sonority, or helping to maintain the ensemble, it was the keyboard part from which the performance was guided. Continuo figures were indispensable, for the soloist performed from a solo part that merely provided cues for entrances—rarely from a full score. Charles Rosen has noted, in fact, that this convention even extended to the concertos of Chopin, which were published with continuo notations.[54] Few such indications, except for the remark *col basso,* have been passed down from Mozart's later concertos, the majority of which were not published during his life, and the nature of Mozart's "conducting part" must remain largely a matter of conjecture. It is clear that the continuo function, however, in no way diminished the integrity of contrast in the opposition of performing forces; the part obviously no longer suggests a basis of composition but rather a new use of a long-established practice. The striking subtleties of its preserved "realizations" further distinguish the Concerto in E-flat Major K. 271. In its merging of symphonic and pianistic attributes, the work marks the highest point of Mozart's pianistic oeuvre during this decade.

✳

The period 1773–81 was a particularly critical period in Mozart's career, and as the travels undertaken during his young manhood left their mark upon his musical development, they shaped the Mozartean pianistic style. We have seen reflections of the Viennese "learned" manner, of the Mannheim idiom, and of a particular Parisian taste in his work. The assimilation was ever subtle, although it included personal influences, such as those of Schuster and Schobert; yet all of it resulted in a transformation of characteristic originality.

Mozart had been involved with composition for the piano in three distinct domains (solo, chamber, and orchestral music), and the resulting developments were to some extent parallel. The solo works show a progress in which an attention to certain characteristics—brilliance, expressiveness, and sonority—stands out. The sonatas for piano and violin represent an integration into a wider scope of Mozart's maturing style. Emerging as true ensemble music, the genre, with its new relationship between instruments, engenders an altogether different approach toward writing for the piano. And commensurate with this advance is an expansion of expression, both emotional and pianistic.

Culminating in the *concertante* interpretation of the pianistic medium are the ensemble compositions and concertos that present skilled handling of pianistic writing against the background of an advanced symphonic style. The first masterpiece in the genre, the Concerto in E-flat Major K. 271, marks the threshold of the fulfillment of Mozart's instrumental style. The most striking function of the pianistic idiom in this concerto is in illuminating the subtleties of symphonic design. As we know, the integrity of the form is forcefully stressed from the very beginning in K. 271 by the unexpected focus on the solo instrument. And the established concerto form is now reflected in piano cadenzas that, while preserving their structural function—the elaboration of the cadence—herald the new significance of motivic development through purely pianistic means, yet within a framework of dramatic instrumental invention that was to carry the symphonic age to one of its peaks in Mozart's concerted piano works.

4

The Vienna Years

✳

The decade spanning the years 1781–91, Mozart's last, stands in sharp contrast to the years of travel. He went to Vienna, and with relatively minor interruptions, his stay became permanent. The incentives his work had received from sojourns in foreign countries gave way to more deeply rooted artistic impulses, and while they guided his work through what appears as a more stable and settled phase of his life, the turbulence that marked the beginning of the Vienna years remained.

✳

In order to understand the abrupt change in the circumstances of Mozart's life, it is necessary to recall the constellation of events that marked the years 1780 and 1781. In November 1780, Mozart, still in the employ of the Archbishop of Salzburg, took leave to travel to Munich for the purpose of finishing his opera *Idomeneo* and overseeing its production. His father and sister joined him for the premiere, and the family remained in the city, which offered him a number of artistically rewarding opportunities, until early March. From Munich Mozart was called to Vienna by the archbishop (who was already in the capital) to attend, with the rest of his employer's assemblage, the festivities for the accession of Joseph II to the Imperial throne.

The archbishop remained in Vienna for most of the spring, requiring Mozart to reside with him and his staff. In contrast to Mozart's experience at Munich, where he was treated with a certain equality by the nobility, the renewed subjection to servitude (Mozart was placed below the valets but above the cook at meals)[1] soon proved intolerable. The archbishop refused Mozart performance opportunities outside his own domain, which might have advanced Mozart in certain Viennese circles, and the tensions between Mozart and the archbishop rose during that spring. On 9 May, following a tempestuous exchange, Mozart asked for release from his service. After a month of ignored petitions, Mozart was discharged in a contemptuous fashion by the archbishop's chamberlain, Count Felix Arco. As a result of this irreconcilable break, Mozart emerged as a young artist freed from the obligations and constraints of provincial Salzburg and one who had renounced the system of aristocratic patronage.

It was a decisive moment in music history. Mozart wrote in a letter to his father dated Vienna, 9 May 1781: "My honor is more precious to me than anything else and I know that it is to you also. Do not be the least bit anxious about me. I am so sure of my success in Vienna that I would have resigned without the slightest reason."[2] There is an element of tragedy in this assertion of independence, for despite Mozart's eminent successes in the ensuing years, he was denied the role he had anticipated, that of the completely independent artist, a role eventually embodied in the popular image of Beethoven. Nonetheless, his newfound artistic freedom resulted in immeasurable gains.

*

The Vienna into which the scene of Mozart's life had shifted presented him with traditions and influences that were to converge in a very special way to find expression in his work. The polyphonic art of the Baroque had stayed alive in the capital, and the era of Johann Joseph Fux (1660–1741) was still felt during the rise of the *style galant*. Ludwig Finscher has commented upon the complex subtleties that resulted from the simultaneous existence of two such contrasting styles. The close relationship between the music of church and court, between the Roman Catholic legacy and the Hapsburg emperors, created an affinity for contrapuntal art in both realms.[3] Fux, the court Kapellmeister, had also served as music director of St. Stephen's Cathedral, and the fashion for counterpoint prevailed at the court of Joseph II, whose resident string quartet ensemble was devoted to the performance of fugues.[4] Mozart was aware of the Emperor's tastes, as one can gather from a letter to his father dated Vienna, 24 March 1781: "Well, my chief object here is to introduce myself to the Emperor in some becoming way, for I am absolutely determined that he shall *get to know me*. I should love to run through my opera [*Idomeneo*] for him and then play a lot of fugues, for that is what he likes."[5]

Fux's famous counterpoint treatise played a special role in linking Mozart's and Haydn's work during these years.[6] But the turn towards a more conscious integration of contrapuntal and *galant* styles in Mozart's writing was prompted less by theoretical precepts than by the model of Haydn's own works. By the end of 1781, Haydn had completed his Op. 33 quartet cycle, and it seems certain that Mozart's careful study of these compositions prompted a singular advance in his chamber music style. Haydn's development of the string quartet genre was a remarkably extended process, and while

Haydn's Op. 20 had already marked a significantly mature phase (one, as noted earlier, that arrested Mozart's attention), it was Haydn's famous quartets Op. 33, composed "in an entirely new and special way" that provided the impetus for Mozart's towering quartet compositions. The quartets Op. 10, composed between 1782 and 1785, were dedicated to Haydn and prefaced with an eloquent and touching letter.[7] Haydn's works suggested to Mozart a model of idiomatic quartet scoring in which all four instruments assume part of the musical discussion, a quartet texture whose polyphonic fabric was ever intensified through motivic development. Mozart wrote, "I have learned from Haydn how to write quartets."[8] Thus, these quartets occupy a pivotal position in Mozart's chamber music. An achievement borne of "long and laborious endeavor,"[9] they usher in a golden age of Mozart's chamber music in which the piano was to assume a central role.

Curiously blended with the influence of Haydn's work was another decisive influence, the music of J. S. Bach that Mozart encountered through the acquaintance of Baron Gottfried van Swieten. The son of the personal physician to the Empress Maria Theresa, van Swieten obtained a wide and informed musical experience through the opportunities of a diplomatic career that took him to Brussels, Paris, and London.[10] His last diplomatic assignment was to prove especially significant because, as Ambassador to Prussia (1770–77), he became familiar with the distinguished musical circle of Princess Anna Amalia, including Friedrich Wilhelm Marpurg and Johann Philipp Kirnberger, the latter the Kapellmeister to the princess as well as one of the most distinguished pupils of J. S. Bach. Having been introduced to the music of the Leipzig cantor, van Swieten returned to Vienna with priceless collections, among them the printed edition of the *Art of Fugue* and manuscript copies of the *Well-Tempered Clavier* and the organ trios. Assuming the duties of prefect of the Imperial Court Library, he held the Sunday matinee gatherings at which, as Mozart reported in April 1782, "nothing is played but Handel and Bach."[11] Einstein speaks of a resulting "revolution and crisis" in Mozart's creative activity.[12] As the baron's "clavier-player," Mozart made arrangements of Bach fugues for van Swieten's string ensemble, also composing new preludes.[13] Thus he was presented, firsthand, not only with a new musical perspective but also with a distinctly different keyboard style; yet Mozart's compositions in response to this stimulus were written for the piano, his "personal instrument of improvisation and experimentation."[14]

STYLE STUDIES

The first major work to reflect Mozart's consuming interest in the style of the late baroque was the Prelude (Fantasy) and Fugue in C Major K. 394 (383a).

Mozart's letter to his sister dated Vienna, 20 April 1782, which described the circumstances, offers a rare glimpse into an astounding process of composition.

> I send you herewith a prelude and a three-part fugue. The reason why I did not reply to your letter at once was that on account of the wearisome labour of writing these small notes, I could not finish the composition any sooner. And even so, it is awkwardly done, for the prelude ought to come first and the fugue to follow. But I composed the fugue first and wrote it down while I was thinking out the prelude. . . . My dear Constanze is really the cause of the fugue's coming into the world. The Baron van Swieten, to whom I go every Sunday, gave me all the works of Handel and Sebastian Bach to take home with me (after I had played them to him). When Constanze heard the fugues, she absolutely fell in love with them. Now she will listen to nothing but fugues, and particularly (in this kind of composition) the works of Handel and Bach. Well, as she had often heard me play fugues out of my head, she asked me if I had ever written any down, and when I said I had not, she scolded me roundly for not recording some of my compositions in this most artistic and beautiful of all musical forms, and never ceased to entreat me until I wrote down a fugue for her. So that is its origin. I have purposely written above it *Andante Maestoso*, as it must not be played too fast. For if a fugue is not played slowly, the ear cannot clearly distinguish the theme when it comes in and consequently the entire effect is missed. In time, and when I have a favourable opportunity, I intend to compose five more and then present them to the Baron van Swieten, whose collection of good music, though small in quantity, is great in quality.[15]

Mozart's exploration of fugal writing goes far beyond a style exercise, although there are plausible associations between Mozart's fugue and one from the *Well-Tempered Clavier*.[16] In terms of keyboard texture, the fugal style involved a technical aspect that at first impression stands isolated in Mozart's work. The combination of two themes, subject and countersubject, in one hand posed a challenge not encountered before in Mozart's keyboard writing. Yet this more intense use of the five fingers of one hand reappears in various guises throughout Mozart's later piano works.

Conversely, an improvisatory keyboard style somewhat reminiscent of Bach's *Chromatic Fantasy* proves to be in fact germane to the existing Mozartean idiom. It is a type of writing we know from Mozart's improvisations, modulating preludes, and the Capriccio. And since van Swieten's manuscript copy of the *Well-Tempered Clavier* was solely a collection of fugues,[17] Mozart clearly had no model in mind for the prelude. The wider pianistic scope of the prelude also lends expression to a typical classical pianoforte style with its repeated chords and passages for crossed hands.

A specific familiarity with the keyboard work of Handel, some of whose music Mozart had already known, also increased as a result of the association with the baron's musical circle. It is manifested not in the strict form of fugue but rather in a type of composition that formed the core of Handel's keyboard work, the clavier suite. The Suite in C Major K. 399 (385i) composed in 1782, though incomplete (consisting of Ouverture, Allemande, Courante, and opening measures of a Sarabande), suggests a keyboard idiom common in the Baroque but particularly associated with Handel's collections of suites issued in 1720.[18] As early as 1800, Mozart's suite was recognized as "being in the style of Handel"[19] (Mozart added no particular title designation in the autograph), and Handel's keyboard style was indeed to prove a significant influence on Mozart.[20]

The writing in this suite is characterized by a contrapuntal texture that stands in contrast to the dense fabric of the fugue. The combination of two contrapuntal voices in one hand is intimated rather than seemingly forced. Still, a certain modernity is evident, in part from the harmonic language; the different tonalities of the Ouverture and its fugal sections, the Allemande, Courante, and Sarabande, outlining a key scheme atypical of Baroque suite design, follow a wider logic of overall organization. Passages in parallel thirds and sixths are not characteristic so much of Handel's as of Mozart's own keyboard style, although the fragmentary beginning of the Sarabande represents a typically Handelian gesture (4.1).

A number of fugue fragments exist, formerly assigned to the year 1782, the principal year of Mozart's preoccupation with the style of the late Baroque. Mozart's plan to write five more fugues, as proposed in the letter to his sister, was part of the basis for this dating. But recent research has shown that while some of these fragments may go back to 1782, a number derive from a later period, some possibly as late as 1789.[21] Mozart's interest in fugue was clearly not an isolated event but a continuing application, and indeed, the fragments may not demonstrate eventually rejected work so much as studies in composition or even "works in progress."[22] The fragments vary, ranging from a few measures to extensive but incomplete compositions (in some cases, they were

4.1. Suite in C Major K. 399 (385i), Sarabande, mm. 1–4

finished by others, such as Maximilian Stadler and Simon Sechter). Most of these works were probably conceived for the piano, though the Fugue in G Minor K. 401 (375e), a work deriving from 1782, may have been intended for the organ (a keyboard duet version also exists).[23]

Mozart's new involvement with the contrapuntal art was to receive its first truly indigenous expression in a medium divorced from the piano but central to his work, the string quartet. The first of the quartets dedicated to Haydn and completed at the end of 1782, one year after Haydn had finished his Op. 33, K. 387 ends in a fugue. Ludwig Finscher has appraised the significance of this work in terms of the Bach inspiration:

> What Mozart strives for here, in the G major quartet KV 387, has the effect of a synthesis of the Haydn quartet style with the experiences gained from the examination of Bach (an examination for which there is no counterpart in Haydn's case), and what is more a synthesis of programmatic design. Double fugue, sonata-style rondo and song melody are exploited in the service of a new, superior goal, but in such a way that they do not lose their singularity for one moment. What remains of the arduous preoccupation with Bach is only the fugal work—so to speak in abstracto—as *one* style medium among others.[24]

Mozart's return to focused contrapuntal expression at the keyboard a year later produced a similarly mature work: the Fugue in C Minor K. 426 for two pianos, dated 29 December 1783.

The theme of the C Minor Fugue begins in octaves, boldly announcing a synthesis of the contrapuntal style of the late Baroque and the classical pianistic idiom. The four-voice fugue represents a work of consummate craftsmanship, and the intensely concentrated manipulation of the subject produces an austere quality that characterizes many later Mozart works written in the minor mode. Yet the skill of its contrapuntal treatment forms part of a total picture in which Mozart's harmonic imagination—in terms of both large-scale design and the use of dissonance for expressive purpose—leads to a work of sublime quality.

Tied to this quality is a style specifically derived from the expressive possibilities of the piano. The distinct character of the subject results partly from a series of "sigh" motifs whose melodic articulation is accentuated by careful marking, and the repeated-note motif and trill of the brief countersubject add to this impression (4.2). The intensity of mood is borne out in octaves at those passages most technically conducive to such doubling. Trills, especially in episodes, transcend the role of ornament, assuming a pianistic brilliance and, through sequential treatment, attaining great dramatic force. In its entirety, the fugue illustrates a pianistic style that requires great independence of the hands. While this four-voice fugue, distributed over two pianos (and four

4.2. Fugue in C Minor K. 426 for two pianos, mm. 1–5

hands), demonstrates greater technical difficulty than the three-voice fugue for piano solo, the difference in difficulty is related to the blending of an unfamiliar texture with an indigenous style. At the fugue's climax, this blending achieves dramatic focus through the juxtaposition of stretti and inversions with orchestral patterns of decidedly symphonic origin.

Beethoven made a copy of this fugue for the purposes of study.[25] Indeed, the Grosse Fuge seems to stand in the tradition established by K. 426. Beethoven may have had a model of medium as well as of form: as late as 1788 Mozart arranged the fugue for string quartet, prefacing it with an Adagio. This transformation, designated as K. 546, shows how highly Mozart must have thought of the original work. The Adagio, one of Mozart's finest attainments in quartet writing, begins with the gesture of a French overture but turns to an afterthought, developed in Mozartean part-writing, that is reminiscent of the famous *Dissonance* Quartet (both its introduction and slow movement) from the set dedicated to Haydn.

WORKS FOR PIANO AND VIOLIN

For Mozart, the decade of the 1780s was as eventful and as astoundingly crowded as that of the 1820s was for Schubert. Mozart's first publication in Vienna, a set of sonatas for piano and violin published as Op. 2,[26] initiates the new phase of his creative career. In distinction to Mozart's earlier works in the genre, these sonatas might truly be designated as chamber music. Mozart's chamber music, in fact, spans the decade, but the chamber music with piano follows a special path. Along with essays for piano and violin are works that, arranged chronologically (the quintet, the two quartets, and the trios), display ever more subtle complexities. While representing a stylistic development that bears the mark of his work in other realms, the chamber music documents a particular aspect of his maturing pianistic style.

While two of the six sonatas from Mozart's Op. 2 were composed earlier, the Sonata in C Major K. 296 at Mannheim in 1778 for his pupil Mlle. Therese-Pierron Serrarius and the Sonata in B-flat Major K. 378 (317d) at Salzburg in 1779 or in 1781 at Munich, the Sonatas in G Major K. 379 (373a), in F Major K. 376 (374d), in F Major K. 377 (374e), and in E-flat Major K. 380 (374f) were written in Vienna during the spring and summer of 1781. The opus was dedicated to Josepha von Auernhammer, a piano pupil of Mozart who was also the dedicatee of the Sonata in D Major K. 448 (375a) for two pianos, composed in November 1781, the month that saw the issue of the series by Artaria. The sonatas generally demonstrate an advance over the earlier ones in style and form and specifically in pianistic writing.

With one exception, they consist of three movements in contrast to the two-movement plan in most of the Mannheim series. A more integral role is assumed by the violin, and this leads to a gradual shift from the exchange of musical material "to true dialogue."[27] A contemporary writer observed the significance and the novelty of the opus: "These sonatas are the only ones of this kind. Rich in new ideas and in evidence of the great musical genius of their author. Very brilliant and suited to the instrument. At the same time the accompaniment of the violin part is so artfully combined with the clavier part that both instruments are kept constantly alert; so that these sonatas require just as skilled a player on the violin as on the clavier."[28] Later in the decade, Mozart wrote four more sonatas for piano and violin, works of ever-increasing complexity, though one is designated *für Anfänger*.

The more intricate combination of the instruments in the statement and development of musical ideas is part of a widened perspective that makes new demands on the keyboard part. Virtuoso figuration in the left hand comparable to that in the right hand now becomes characteristic. The expanded sonority prompts a different pianistic approach: broken-chord accompaniment of greater scope now complements the melodic design; thick chord textures in both hands become prevalent as an idiom in alternation with the violin part; and the exploitation of the bass register and indeed the entire range of the keyboard establishes an altogether different pianistic expression, brilliant but at the same time wholly consistent with a chamber music ideal. Perhaps the most dramatic example of a new conception of sonority is demonstrated in the opening of the Sonata in G Major K. 379 (373a). Not only does the fullness of the opening rolled chords in the piano announce a distinct style, but it summons a change in technique that is carried through in an extended arpeggio accompaniment during the thematic statement of the violin. The arpeggio pattern, when transferred to the bass and combined with the repeated motif in the melody, goes far in suggesting the keyboard style of Beethoven or Schubert. Other passages that appear as harbingers of nineteenth-century pianistic technique are found in the Sonata in E-flat Major K. 380 (374f), where writing in the low register combines with repeated chords to form an accompaniment marked by expressive *sforzati* in both hands (4.3).

The unusual form and range of mood of the Sonata in G Major K. 379 (373a) may have been prompted by the circumstances surrounding its composition and first performance. It was composed shortly after Mozart's arrival in Vienna for one of the archbishop's gatherings and was performed by Mozart and Gaetano Brunetti on an evening in which, as Mozart wrote, he might have earned an amount equal to half of his yearly Salzburg salary, had the archbishop permitted him to perform before the Emperor instead,[29] and the very genesis of the sonata is remarkable: "Today (for I am writing at eleven o'clock at night) we had a concert, where three of my compositions were performed—new ones, of course, a rondo for a concerto for Brunetti; a sonata with violin accompaniment for myself, which I composed last night between eleven and twelve (but in order to finish it, I only wrote the accompaniment for Brunetti and retained my own part in my head)."[30] The variations of the second movement, forming such a marked contrast to the first movement,

4.3. Sonata in E-flat Major K. 380 (374f) for piano and violin, 2d movement, mm. 15–19

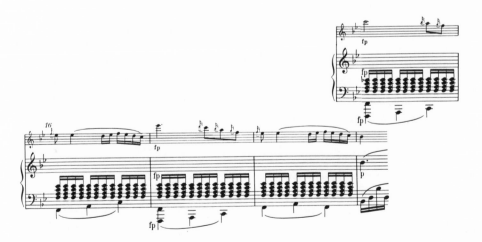

display a demanding intricacy of part-writing for the piano. In the first variation for piano alone, the spacing of voices requires both hands to share in the
realization of an integral voice. At the same time, the left hand is called upon
to stretch the interval of a tenth. Increasing demands on pianistic technique
were to follow in Mozart's last large-scale Sonatas for Piano and Violin in B-
flat Major K. 454, in E-flat Major K. 481, and in A Major K. 526.

Three additional sonatas for piano and violin are linked to the year 1782.
The Sonatas in A Major K. 402 (385e) and in C Major K. 403 (385c) date with
certainty from August and September 1782, while the Sonata in C Major K.
404 (385d) was written either in 1782 or 1788.[31] K. 402 (385e), with its concluding fugue, as well as K. 403 (385c), may have been written with Constanze
in mind, and it is interesting that, like other compositions intended for her,
such as the Mass in C Minor K. 427 (417a) dating from the period July 1782
to May 1783, the works in this group remained incomplete (Maximilian
Stadler later provided completions). In chronological order, the works follow
the Auernhammer set of 1781 and precede Mozart's last three large-scale compositions in the genre. Being fragments they also contrast with the other sonatas by their more modest formal design and content.

The fugue in the Sonata in A Major serves as a special reminder of Constanze's interest in the form. While essentially still a style exercise, the intricate
work demonstrates a keyboard style quite idiomatic to the piano. One per-
ceives for the first time a fluent pianistic expression of the austere contrapuntal
fabric.

But particularly striking is the totally different Andante, ma un poco adagio
that precedes the fugue: it bears many traits of an advanced pianistic style
found also in the Auernhammer set. An unusually rich texture assumes prominence: repeated chords (especially in the middle register) form patterns that
are reflected in passages of double-stops for the violin, and the coloristic effects of widely spaced registers are also stressed. Once again, this "prelude"
exhibits a pianistic language more readily associated with Beethoven and
Schubert. The surprising contrast expressed in the pairing of the two movements exhibits the full range of piano sonority characteristic of this period in
Mozart's work.

The three Sonatas in B-flat Major K. 454, in E-flat Major K. 481, and in A
Major K. 526 for piano and violin stand as crowning achievements in the
genre. Composed in the years 1784, 1785, and 1787, respectively, they reflect
significant points in Mozart's career marked by other aspects of his work.
Principal among them is the form of the concerto, which by the spring of 1784
had arrived at a new maturity. In the same month in which Mozart wrote the

Sonata in B-flat Major K. 454, he had completed the Piano Concerto in G Major K. 453, which is exemplary of a highly advanced orchestral style. By July 1783, Mozart had composed the first three string quartets in the series dedicated to Haydn. Thus the period of these final piano-violin sonatas is characterized by Mozart's increasing mastery of other forms.

In these works, the violin is placed on an entirely equal footing with the piano. The blending of instruments reflects Mozart's ever-growing commitment to the form of the concerto, and in the assimilation of the orchestral idiom the ensemble sonata gains final stature. Especially sophisticated treatment is given to various structures. Striking is the set of variations forming the finale of the Sonata in E-flat Major K. 481 and the large sonata-rondo closing the Sonata in A Major K. 526. The harmonic language reaches unusual expression in the modulations of the Adagio in the Sonata in E-flat Major K. 481.

Like that of the Concerto in E-flat Major K. 271, the origin of the Sonata in B-flat Major K. 454 involved a famous performer, the violin virtuoso Regina Strinasacchi, whose gift may have served as an important incentive. Mozart wrote in a letter dated Vienna, 24 April 1784: "We now have here the famous Strinasacchi from Mantua, a very good violinist. She has a great deal of taste and feeling in her playing. I am this moment composing a sonata which we are going to play together on Thursday at her concert in the theatre."[32] Mozart, not having taken time to write out the piano part, performed the sonata at its premiere with a blank manuscript before him, to which he added the part only later.[33]

The equality of partners is announced in a grand opening gesture. After a lyrical answer presented alternately by the two instruments, the piano part shifts totally to the hushed orchestral expression of the dramatic *scena* for the next statement, which turns into pianistic brilliance as the roles are again exchanged (4.4). Bravura pianistic writing borders on that of a concerto cadenza. But the new concentration on the motivic phrase, the finely drawn articulation and expressive marking within the contrapuntal fabric pose ever-greater demands on the independence of both hands (4.5).

The Sonata in A Major K. 526 is probably Mozart's greatest achievement in the genre, a work to which Beethoven's *Kreutzer* Sonata has been compared. The seemingly mechanical brilliance of the keyboard figuration in the last movement (written in a *perpetuum mobile* fashion for the right hand) actually hides very subtle motivic and melodic details. The challenge to pianistic technique lies in adjusting to a surprising complexity within the presto tempo. It seems doubly surprising, given the inherent character of the parts, but one is faced not with a simple three-part texture so much as with compositional thought created by highly independent part-writing.

4.4. Sonata in B-flat Major K. 454 for piano and violin, 1st movement, mm. 5–9

4.5. Sonata in B-flat Major K. 454 for piano and violin, 1st movement, mm. 98–105

LARGER CHAMBER MUSIC WORKS

"I composed two grand concertos and then a quintet, which called forth the very greatest applause: I myself consider it to be the best work I have ever composed. It is written for one oboe, one clarinet, one horn, one bassoon and the pianoforte. How I wish you could have heard it! And how beautifully it was performed!"[34] Mozart wrote these words to his father in a letter dated Vienna, 19 April 1784 about the Quintet in E-flat Major K. 452, a work composed in March 1784 that opened a new phase in the history of chamber music as it did in Mozart's own oeuvre. The Sonata in B-flat Major K. 454 was written less than a month after the quintet; two piano quartets and six piano trios followed within the next four years.

The turn to chamber music in Mozart's pianistic work might be interpreted as an expression of his new and powerful interest in polyphony. The variety of timbres and idioms inherent in the woodwind ensemble is now placed in the service of independent part-writing. The different roles develop heightened personal character, as in Mozart's dramatic work, and the blend of individual elements is governed by counterpoint.

The opening tutti chords of the quintet's introductory Largo initiate, in ever fuller textures, a keyboard style in which the piano balances four other instruments through mercurial shifts in matching and contrasting sonorities. The alternation between chords and lyrical motif in the beginning, emphasized by *forte* and *piano*, point up an unprecedented flexibility of the pianistic medium. The keyboard style varies with the piano's ever-changing role of stating solo material, providing accompaniment, or sharing motivic work. Particularly characteristic is the transparency stemming from contrapuntal synthesis of the instrumental sound (4.6).

As part of the quintet setting, the piano offers a "voice" to the ensemble by a pianistic tone color often achieved through doublings at the third, sixth, octave, or tenth. This type of doubling, hitherto largely absent from Mozart's keyboard writing, shows a special refinement of the pianistic timbre: the piano assumes the character of the woodwinds (4.7). As will be seen in the discussion of his development of the woodwind writing in the concertos, Mozart's inclination toward woodwind sonorities may have been prompted by the tradition of the woodwind ensemble, or *Harmonie*, in the Vienna of Joseph II. Moreover, by virtue of its design—notably its leather-covered, hollow wooden hammers, its relatively thin strings, and its all-wood construction—Mozart's instrument produced a sound that merges remarkably with that of the woodwind instruments. It even bore an acoustic affinity to contemporary string

4.6. Quintet in E-flat Major K. 452 for piano and winds, 1st movement, mm. 56–60

timbre in the distinct overtones that resulted from the harmonics and fundamentals of the fortepiano's characteristic tone.[35]

Dynamic indications, extensive in this score, are now subject to a different subtlety. The woodwind *fp* gives way to more precise expression in the piano part, or a crescendo begun by the winds leads through a *forte* entrance of the piano to a *subito piano*. In short, contrasts are employed in moments of distinctive surprise. A climactic point, both in the structure of the work and the blend of its ensemble, is reached in the cadenza for the final movement. The cadenza loses its improvisatory character. It is not an added flourish that might

4.7. Quintet in E-flat Major K. 452 for piano and winds, 1st movement, mm. 44–49

have been executed either by the piano or oboe but pure motivic development in six moving parts. The keyboard writing reflects this integrity in a piano part that combines a finely reserved approach with typical Mozartean brilliance.

Like the quintet for piano and winds, the two Quartets for Piano and Strings in G Minor K. 478 and in E-flat Major K. 493, composed in October 1785 and June 1786, respectively, largely establish a new genre of chamber music. Mozart had planned to write three piano quartets for the Viennese publisher Franz Anton Hoffmeister. As Nissen reports, the G Minor Quartet, once published, was judged too difficult by the public, and plans for the series were abandoned. "Mozart voluntarily released him [Hoffmeister] from the contract."[36] However a second piano quartet was composed the following year and was published by Artaria.

The Vienna public may have been startled by the piano's complex role as part of a new ensemble. The strings suggest the flexible medium of the string quartet as exemplified in Mozart's *Haydn* Quartets. The last of these was completed in January 1785, but all of them proved too difficult to be widely performed at first.[37] In the piano quartets, thematic material is stated separately in the strings and unfolded either jointly or successively in the piano and string parts. Yet at times the piano merely adds touches of color to the string ensemble, as if providing an orchestral bass. In other passages, the piano expresses a larger orchestral palette: after a solo statement of the opening theme for the Andante of the G Minor Quartet, the strings take up the subject, and the piano part suggests the addition of winds in a symphonic tutti. In the second movement of the G Minor Quartet, a striking reflection of the variety of ensemble constellations is a passage placing a cantilena in the piano against a fully worked-out string texture, the simplicity of the piano's single melodic lines resulting in a highly expressive solo. By contrast, in the coda for the first movement of the G Minor Quartet, the keyboard part becomes a veritable orchestral tutti while providing, within its brilliant tremolo patterns, a melodic answer to the statement of the strings.

Whereas the piano assumes the dominant role in the dramatic opening of the G Minor Quartet, it shares the gravely dramatic gestures of the string ensemble in florid octave passages leading to the recapitulation of its first movement. The integrated part writing gains a particular significance in both closing movements. A sustained trill provides the "cadenza" effect leading to the final statement of the rondo theme in the G Minor Quartet. In the development of the Larghetto in the E-flat Major Quartet, the expressive figuration in the upper register of the piano stands against a string texture articulated by imitative entries; its expressiveness arises from subtle details of melodic design (as well as harmonic and dynamic effects). The subtleties are analogous to the pattern found in the opening of the Rondo to the Sonata in A Major K. 526 for piano and violin, though in a contrapuntally richer ensemble setting.

In contrast to the quintet and quartets, the piano trios may be viewed against the background of a typical eighteenth-century form. The combination of violin, cello, and keyboard instrument (the harpsichord or organ) had become characteristic of sonata settings of the late Baroque. As can be seen in Joseph Haydn's early trios, this scoring gained new scope, but the new ensemble texture reflected an established practice: the cello supported the left hand of the keyboard part.[38] Haydn's interest in the piano trio extended, with certainty, from 1784 until 1797, and a number of works have been attributed to him that could place his involvement with the genre as early as 1760. It is interesting that, with the exception of three trios composed in 1790, his works are entitled sonatas (the early compositions for harpsichord, violin, and bass attributed to Haydn bear the designation of divertimento or partita—even concerto and capriccio).[39] His continued cultivation of the genre outlined a particular course that in some instances clearly suggests external influences (notably that of the group of pianist-composers known as the London Pianoforte School).[40] Still, in the last trios, composed during and after Haydn's second visit to England (1794–95), the writing now begins to exhibit, especially in terms of pianistic texture, the influence of Mozart on his work.

As has been mentioned, Mozart's Op. 3, the sonatas for keyboard and violin or flute with optional cello (K. 11–15), composed in 1764, occupy a special position in Mozart's oeuvre. While they continue the style established in the accompanied sonatas of his Op. 1 and Op. 2, the inclusion of a cello part— optional use of a cello in performance was customary even without a separately written-out part—suggests the inception of the piano trio scoring. Mozart was not to return to the genre until twelve years later, when in the summer of 1776, still at Salzburg, he composed the Divertimento in B-flat Major K. 254. In this work, written less than a year before Mozart's Mannheim sonatas for piano and violin, Mozart's writing approaches the genuine ensemble exchange of thematic material. At the same time, the cello assumes a new role. While mostly providing a support for the bass line, its doubling is handled more imaginatively, taking advantage of the variety in color in different registers of the instrument, and the cello part begins to state motifs or themes independently of the keyboard part.

The shift to a perfected chamber music style in the genre of the piano trio occurred ten years later in 1786 after Mozart had completed the second of his two quartets for piano and strings. The new works in G Major K. 496, E-flat Major K. 498, and B-flat Major K. 502 present a trio texture of unrivaled integrity. It is revealing that Mozart designated them as *terzets*.[41] It is also significant that, among the three trios completed in 1786, the second was written for piano, clarinet, and viola, an ensemble in itself suggesting a highly complex approach. Three more trios followed in 1788, the Trios in E Major K. 542, C Major K. 548, and G Major K. 564.

The keyboard writing in the Trio in E-flat Major K. 498, the *Kegelstatt* Trio, bears a certain resemblance to that found in the quintet for piano and winds. This may result, in part, from the presence of the clarinet and the subtle adjustment Mozart made for the novel instrumentation. A certain intimate quality, suggestive of the divertimento spirit, is stressed both in the instrumentation and in the order and type of movements: the opening Andante in 6/8 time, the Minuet, and the closing Rondeau in allegretto tempo. Mozart was especially fond of the clarinet, as he was of the viola, and circumstances of composition indicate that the work may have been written expressly for a Viennese family, the Jacquins, to whom Mozart was especially close. (At one performance at the Jacquin home, Mozart himself played the viola part and Anton Stadler the clarinet, the piano part probably being assumed by Mlle. Franziska Jacquin, a piano pupil of Mozart.)[42] The score combines the instruments in a chamber music style distinctly different from that of the other trios of 1786. The viola takes an active role in the texture, more so than in the piano quartets. In blending with the woodwind quality of melodic contour, color, and character, the pianistic medium proves again a particularly well-suited partner.

The composition of the last series of trios is clearly marked by the last phase of Mozart's work, which is also reflected in the last two Concertos for Piano and Orchestra in D Major K. 537 and B-flat Major K. 595, as well as in the last solo works for piano. Minor keys are given wider use, and there are striking key relationships and juxtapositions of major and minor tonalities. The cello part shows greater independence throughout the series. It represents a more varied range from bass to tenor and frequently assumes the focus in the ensemble.

Once again, the new character prompts an enlarged palette of pianistic expressiveness and sonority. Greater refinement of dynamic expression is characteristically indicated by the marking *mfp* in the slow movement of the Trio in C Major K. 548. The use of the Alberti bass in a lower register is novel and calls to mind a sonority associated with Beethoven, as do the virtuoso passages in the first movement. By contrast, the initial *dolce* of the third movement of the Trio in E Major K. 542, with its broken-chord accompaniment or "oscillating bass" employed in middle register, characterizes an opening phrase of typical Mozartean grace but one that places a new demand on pianistic technique through the addition of an inner voice. The blend of simplicity of character and complexity of pianistic execution increasingly becomes a distinguishing trait in this phase of Mozart's work, as does an increasing economy of means. It becomes apparent as such in the chronological sequence of piano quintet, piano quartet, and piano trio. The trios conclude this chapter in Mozart's work, signifying the stage of final maturity in a genre that began, significantly, with what he called "the best work I have ever composed."

CONCERTOS

Mozart cultivated the concerto for violin industriously, but only for a short time; to the concerto for single wind instruments—flute, oboe, bassoon, horn, clarinet—and the *sinfonia concertante*, he devoted only intermittent, though at times very serious, attention; but with the piano he concerned himself from earliest youth until the end, and undoubtedly we should have had more than just two piano concertos dating from the last four or five years of his life—we might have had ten or twelve such masterpieces—if the Vienna public had paid greater attention to Mozart than it did.[43]

As we have observed, the concerto form occupied Mozart's attention as early as 1767 when he made the arrangements known as the *Pasticcio* Concertos."[44] Prior to this, Mozart had performed concertos at home and on the tours. Johann Andreas Schachter, family friend and trumpeter at the Salzburg court, related an anecdote of the child's having attempted, apparently with some success, the composition of a concerto at the age of four or five.[45] The concerto arrangements of sonatas by J. C. Bach followed in 1771 or 1772; the Concerto in D Major K. 175, Mozart's first totally original concerto, in 1773; a group of three concertos, one of which was for three pianos, in 1776; and the singularly important Concerto in E-flat Major K. 271 in 1777. The Concerto for Two Pianos in E-flat Major K. 365 (316a) was written in Salzburg in 1779 after Mozart's tour to cities in southern Germany and Paris, which had begun two years earlier in 1777.

With Mozart's move to Vienna, a decisive new phase of his work in the concerto form began, and the genre underwent a development similar to that characterizing the genre of the Mozartean symphony in the preceding decade. In fact, Mozart's seventeen concertos written over the years 1782–91 summarize the achievement of his instrumental ideal.[46]

The works may be divided into series according to the dates and circumstances of composition.

1782–83:	A Major K. 414 (385p)
	F Major K. 413 (387a)
	C Major K. 415 (387b)
1784:	E-flat Major K. 449
	B-flat Major K. 450
	D Major K. 451
	G Major K. 453
	B-flat Major K. 456
	F Major K. 459
1785–86:	D minor K. 466
	C Major K. 467
	E-flat Major K. 482
	A Major K. 488
	C Minor K. 491
	C Major K. 503
1788:	D Major K. 537
1788–91:	B-flat Major K. 595

The concertos were composed primarily with Mozart's own appearances before the Viennese public in mind. Mozart's keen judgment of the Viennese public is suggested by the nature of the first group of concertos, composed in 1782 and early 1783. They were intended specifically to gain success in the subscription performances and were also designed to be successful commercially by virtue of an orchestration of decided flexibility, as Mozart stated in a famous letter to his father dated Vienna, 28 December 1782:

> There are still two concertos wanting to make up the series of subscription concertos. These concertos are a happy medium between what is too easy and too difficult; they are very brilliant, pleasing to the ear, and natural, without being vapid. There are passages here and there from which the connoisseurs alone can derive satisfaction; but these passages are written in such a way that the less learned cannot fail to be pleased, though without knowing why.[47]

In a letter to the Parisian music publisher J. C. Sieber dated Vienna, 26 April 1783, he wrote: "Well, this letter is to inform you that I have three piano concertos ready, which can be performed with full orchestra, namely with oboes and horns, or merely *a quattro*."[48] At the time of the first letter, it is evident that Mozart had completed only one concerto, the Concerto in A Major K. 414 (385p). The other concertos in the group bear a certain similarity to it, particularly with respect to the optional wind parts. Yet it should be noted that while the Concerto in F Major K. 413 (387a), like the Concerto in A Major, calls for the traditional wind complement of oboes and horns, the more brilliant Concerto in C Major K. 414 (387b) calls for a pair of bassoons, trumpets, and timpani. Though the absence of the winds may not affect the integrity of part-writing, it clearly results in a loss of expressive tone color. Since within these series of concertos there is variety and a range of character and since Mozart sought to appeal to the amateur as well as the connoisseur (thus securing a wider audience for his works), a scoring for piano quintet was highly desirable.

A notable increase in bravura writing, particularly in the first-movement development section, characterizes these concertos, partly indicating Mozart's awareness of the dramatic tension inherent in the form. The virtuoso writing heightens the expressive quality of the modulations, and this emphasizes their function in the overall structure. A considerable variety is demonstrable in these first three Viennese concertos. Even the Concerto in F Major (with its unusual first movement in triple meter), which places modest demands on pianistic technique, requires cross-hand technique, whereas the Concerto in C Major, which maintains a brilliant style throughout, makes special demands on the soloist's skill in the imitative passages at the beginning of the development.

A stylistic feature established in these concertos is the soloistic statement of one or more themes in the exposition of the first movement. Such thematic statements, generally lyrical in quality, are characteristically presented in the middle and upper registers of the piano. They often initiate more brilliant passages leading to the cadence at the exposition's conclusion. The more prominent presence of the orchestra prompts an enlivened pianistic texture, with varying phrase lengths stressing certain harmonic patterns. These phrases of brilliant figuration are distinguished by rhythmic acceleration and an enlarged keyboard range.

Mozart quotes a theme of J. C. Bach (from the overture Bach composed for the opera *La calamità dei cuori*) in the Andante of the Concerto in A Major K. 414 (385p).[49] Its use may have been intended as a gesture, for J. C. Bach had died on New Year's Day, 1782. This Andante, on a larger scale than previous middle movements in the piano concertos, contains a fully worked-out sonata form whose development leads to a recapitulation in the corresponding minor key by way of an expressive *Eingang* or lead-in. Both this passage and the cadenza are marked by a level of technical difficulty normally associated with opening or closing movements. The cadenza, moreover, blends florid passage work with thematic and motivic development.

As various biographical facts indicate, the year 1784 may be considered one of the most productive and successful, indeed happy, periods in Mozart's life. He was in demand as a soloist by the Viennese and was heard frequently as performer in his own "Akademie" concertos. During the particularly success-ful Lenten concert season of 1784, he appeared nineteen times in one month. Concurrent with these appearances was the rather astonishing accomplish-ment of the composition of four piano concertos over a period of two months, the Concertos in E-flat Major K. 449, B-flat Major K. 450, D Major K. 451, and G Major K. 453. Both the Concertos in B-flat Major and D Major (as well as the Quintet for Piano and Winds in E-flat Major K. 452) were written during March. Two more concertos were written later in 1784, the Concertos in B-flat Major K. 456 and F Major K. 459.

The Concerto in E-flat Major K. 449 initiates a highly mature series of concertos, although its orchestration is still written with a view toward omit-ting the winds in a manner similar to that of the concertos written in 1782–83.[50] A varied texture stressing strong contrasts between soloist and orchestra is apparent throughout and places this concerto in a line of evolution emanat-ing from the Concerto in E-flat Major K. 271. Like the first movement of K. 271, the opening movement of K. 449 is tightly constructed and gains considerable coherence through the development of an initial motif. The con-trapuntal finale suggests a comparison with the canonic movement in the

Concerto in D Major K. 175, composed eleven years earlier. The movement opens in a contrapuntal texture that combines two distinct themes. These become the basis of the movement, a circumstance that has prompted suggestions of a Haydn influence.[51] Yet the pianistic style remains characteristically Mozartean and is evident in the melodic transformation of the principal subject in statements that are embellished, varied by articulation, presented in octave passages, and in the coda, transformed to a different meter. Ultimately, the contrapuntal idiom finds full expression in a rich fugal texture that involves elaborations of this subject, including its simultaneous inversion. Significantly, the concerto forms the first entry in Mozart's personal catalog of works, *Verzeichnüss aller meiner Werke*, begun in 1784.

With the Concertos in B-flat Major K. 450 and D Major K. 451, the woodwind parts become an essential feature of the orchestral fabric, affecting both the orchestral and pianistic textures: "The orchestra is treated symphonically, with dialogue among its own members, and this leads naturally to a more brilliant treatment of the piano part."[52] In fact, these two concertos are among Mozart's pianistically most elaborate works, the B-flat Concerto possibly being the most difficult of Mozart's concertos in terms of pianistic technique. Striking are the extensive passages for the left hand that show the same degree of difficulty as those for the right hand, as well as passages in the last movement (the first to include the flute in the woodwind group) calling for an especially adroit cross-hand technique in patterns of unusual rhythmic complexity. The challenge to the pianist is multiform: it involves crossing of the left hand over the right in a close position (intertwining or *eindringen*) that emphasizes certain notes in a syncopated pattern, the return crossing to octaves in the bass, and the required fast execution. Indeed, such passages and others like it call to mind Mozart's own description of these concertos as works that "are bound to make the performer perspire."[53]

Elaborations of solo passages, which differed from Mozart's original realizations, are preserved in the parts for the concertos in E-flat Major K. 449 and D Major K. 451 and are notated partly in the hand of Nannerl. These phrases suggest performance possibilities that either enrich the melodic line or enhance the contours in passagework. Particularly telling are the *Extra Manieren* that Mozart provided for measures 56–63 in the second movement of the Concerto in D Major K. 451, which are published in the *NMA* edition of this work. Mozart himself referred to this passage in a letter of 9 June 1784 to his father: "She [Nannerl] is quite right in saying that there is something missing in the solo passage in C in the Andante of the concerto in D. I will supply the deficiency as soon as possible and send it with the cadenzas."[54]

Mozart composed the Concertos in B-flat and D Major specifically for his own use in the Vienna subscription concerts, and the degree of bravura provides clear indications of Mozart's remarkable pianistic virtuosity. But the Concerto in E-flat Major K. 449 had been composed for his student Barbara Ployer, and Mozart himself pointed out its different nature to his father and sister:

> From the point of view of difficulty the B-flat concerto [K. 450] beats the one in D [K. 451]. Well, I am very curious to hear which of those in B-flat, D and G [K. 453] you and my sister prefer. The one in E-flat [K. 449] does not belong at all to the same category. It is of a quite peculiar kind, composed rather for a small orchestra than for a large one. So it is really only a question of the three grand concertos. . . . Of course it is necessary to hear all three well performed and with all the parts.[55]

In fact, Nannerl was to play the Concertos in E-flat Major K. 449 and in D Major K. 451 in Salzburg. The Concerto in G Major K. 453, mentioned in the above letter, was also composed for Barbara Ployer, but as Mozart described, it was to be included among the series of "grand" concertos. A more developed orchestral writing is evident in the more intricate use of the woodwinds: they state, for the first time, much of the thematic material. An enrichment of the symphonic texture leads to refinements in the concerto plan: passages of brilliant figuration in the piano are tied to thematic elaboration and development by the orchestra. While placing more modest demands on pianistic technique than the previous two concertos, this work demonstrates a finer integration of soloist and orchestra, approaching a chamber music style, particularly in the blending of woodwinds and piano and in the sharing of thematic material. Interestingly, this concerto, in which the woodwinds play such a significantly new role, is preceded by the quintet for piano and winds, a work that, as noted, maintains the independence and character of each instrument in a varied texture of assured polyphonic integrity; the exchanges of solo instrument and orchestra now seem to prompt a contrapuntal texture not found in his chamber music.

The third movement of this concerto contains the first instance of a variation set used as a finale. It shows a formal scheme similar to that found in Mozart's independent sets of piano variations, that is, a theme with variations contrasting in key or mode, tempo, and meter. There are five variations followed by an extensive presto coda of a decided opera buffa character. Especially striking is the *minore* variation with its chromatically colored and syncopated melody and its novel use of leaps (4.8).

The Concerto in B-flat Major K. 456 and the Concerto in F Major K. 459 were written in September and December 1784, respectively. The former was intended for a blind virtuoso pianist, Maria Theresia von Paradis. In style and character it is close to the G Major Concerto. The latter continues the

4.8. Concerto in G Major K. 453, 3d movement, mm. 104–12

symphonic approach of the other concertos and, like most of them, concludes with an expansive sonata-rondo. Yet even greater weight is placed in this movement on contrapuntal writing manifest in fugato tutti episodes and in passages pitting the solo part against an imitative texture in the orchestra.

With the Concerto in D Minor K. 466, composed in February 1785 only two months after the Concerto in F Major K. 459, and a companion work, the Concerto in C Major K. 467, written in March 1785, Mozart's involvement with the concerto begins a new phase. These compositions arise from the background of the symphonic concerto form that Mozart had developed in the works of 1784, which assign a greatly strengthened role to the orchestra. They initiate a series of six concertos, three composed in 1785 and three in 1786 that, because of certain stylistic similarities, may be more appropriately grouped in pairs. They are distinguished by a new degree of expressive intensity that is particularly apparent in the D Minor Concerto, Mozart's first concerto in a minor key. Its passionate quality was to make it one of the most popular of Mozart's concertos during the nineteenth century. The work's stature is suggested by Beethoven's composition of cadenzas for its first and third movements, cadenzas that are generally used in performance today.

Both concertos depart in details of form from those of the 1784 series. Much of the thematic material assigned to the orchestra remains its sole province. The urgent, brooding, opening subject of the D Minor Concerto is totally orchestral in idiom and texture and, by its nature, seems not given to pianistic realization, in contrast to the works of 1784 in which there is a strict correspondence between the opening theme of the orchestral introduction and the solo exposition. Conversely, the piano exposition opens with a theme, almost recitative-like in nature, which is later the basis for a development that remains the exclusive domain of the solo instrument. The contrast in assignment of thematic material paradoxically leads to greater unity among the concerto partners, and this integration is borne out in pianistic expression. While never taking up the opening material literally, the piano part in its elaborate figurations accompanies and at the same time transforms the orchestral theme.

Examination of the manner in which Mozart utilized the concerto forces provides special insight into Mozart's manipulation of contemporary sonorities and Mozart's very careful consideration of the strengths and weaknesses of the contemporary instrument. In the opening passage described above, the steadily rising treble of the solo part suggests an element of crescendo that in some measure is stressed by the dropping out of the woodwinds from the orchestral texture; later, the mounting "crescendo" in the piano part expands to full chords in the treble and broken octaves in the bass. Finally, the total sonority culminates, two bars later, in a tutti to which the solo part surrenders.

The passage provides a glimpse into contemporary performance practice. Mozart's consummate expertise in writing for piano and orchestra allows the relatively weak-sounding fortepiano full advantage within the dramatic context of the concerto form.

Indeed, the greater demands for pianistic expression that Mozart made in this work were met in part by the use of a pedal-piano, evidence of which is found in the autograph and designated in the *NMA* edition of this work.[56] Leopold Mozart wrote to his daughter from Vienna on 12 March 1785: "Since my arrival your brother's fortepiano has been taken at least a dozen times to the theatre or to some other house. He has had a large fortepiano pedal made, which stands under the instrument and is about two feet longer and extremely heavy."[57]

In the presentation of secondary and more lyrical subjects in the first movement, the merging of the piano part with the orchestra leads to a simplification of the pianistic texture. But the grander symphonic dimensions and the emotional tone of the work also prompt a pianistic style typically expressed in various octave patterns (4.9). Even the presentation of the second theme is enriched by sweeping pianistic gestures. Momentum is gained from the repe-

4.9. Concerto in D Minor K. 466, 1st movement, mm. 227–30

tition of figurations punctuated by dynamic accents. Particularly striking are the ascending scale patterns in token of a cadenza against the sustained harmonies in the orchestra and leading into a cadential trill. The prolongation of the six-four harmony, itself an expression of dramatic intensity and a feature increasingly developed by Mozart in these years, gains particular definition through the virtuoso pianistic idiom.

The lyrical theme of the second movement, Romanze, is enhanced by an accompaniment that exploits the expressive qualities of the piano's different registers and that is written predominantly in two distinct voices, one mostly in a duet with the orchestral melody, that present special technical demands for the left hand. A rich sonority is derived from sustaining the lowest voice against eighth-note patterns (4.10). The impassioned episode in G minor draws upon the most extensively developed cross-hand technique. It includes passages covering, within two-measure phrases, the entire range of Mozart's piano. While extremely dramatic, this is not the first time that Mozart has covered the complete compass of the instrument; a somewhat similar instance can be seen in the B-flat Concerto K. 450 composed in 1784 (first movement, at the cadence extending over measures 84 and 85.) In the latter example, the left hand is required to cross over the right hand to the top of the keyboard,

4.10. Concerto in D Minor K. 466, 2d movement, mm. 1–4

yet at another passage, in the execution of octaves, the left hand is taxed with almost greater technical difficulty. Long before Beethoven, Mozart drove pianistic technique to the limits of the instrument.

In the Rondo (Allegro assai) the expression of the pianistic idiom itself, in varied characteristic figurations, becomes contrapuntal. Similar though more elaborate patterns stress the climax of the development in the first movement (Allegro maestoso) of the Concerto in C Major K. 467. The treatment of formal outline and contrasting thematic material for the orchestral introduction and solo exposition is comparable in both concertos, although in the C Major Concerto, solo and orchestra blend in broader symphonic design.

The merging of orchestra and solo grows in scope in the Andante of the C Major Concerto: the orchestral setting of the opening theme is suggested by the solo part and leads to an expressive cantilena that gains in color by the pizzicati of the string accompaniment but also by the bold pianistic melody, which involves a crossing leap of more than three octaves into the bass register. Similarly striking is the melodic pairing of the solo instrument with string and winds in the statement of a closing motif that points to a new synthesis of instrumental sound. This integration is stressed in a passage of the Rondo (Allegro vivace assai) where the piano part, in figurations symphonic in nature, assumes the lead and, in a sense, the orchestral role in the exchange and development of the opening motif.

The Concertos in E-flat Major K. 482 and A Major K. 488, composed in December 1785 and March 1786, respectively, approximate more closely the formal plan of the concertos of 1784 in their correspondence of thematic material for orchestra and solo parts. Written during the period in which Mozart was largely occupied with the composition of *The Marriage of Figaro*, they clearly show a more conservative approach than had either of the previous concertos: "The first two [the Concertos in E-flat Major and A Major] give us the impression that he felt he had perhaps gone too far, had given the Viennese public credit for too much, and overstepped the boundaries of 'social' music— or more simply stated, that he saw the favor of the public waning, and sought to win it back with works that would be sure of success."[58] Nonetheless, it is evident that the development of the Mozartean piano concerto continues in these works. "In the A major concerto Mozart again succeeded in meeting his public half-way without sacrificing anything of his own individuality."[59]

These concertos share an instrumentation that now includes the clarinet. As we know, Mozart held a particular affection for the clarinet. It was the woodwind instrument singled out by him for use in some of his most mature chamber music works, the *Kegelstatt* Trio K. 498 (1786), and the Quintet in A Major K. 581 (1789) for clarinet and strings, as well as for his last concerto, the Clarinet Concerto in A Major K. 622, completed less than two months before his death. The addition of the clarinet seems to prompt a generally more complex use of the woodwinds and expansion of orchestral color: there is a remarkable moment in the opening of the E-flat Concerto where the bassoons, against a counterpoint in the horns, assume the second phrase of the melody. And tied to this use of the woodwinds are gestures of sonority that blend the woodwind instruments with the piano (and the woodwinds with the strings) in a new fashion.

H. C. Robbins Landon argues persuasively that the tradition for wind bands in Vienna (the so-called *Harmonie* and, in particular, the emperor's Imperial wind band) and the cultivation of a literature for them decisively affected Mozart's orchestral scoring.[60] Indeed, the use of the woodwind ensemble is notable in the second movement of the Concerto in E-flat Major K. 482, where in certain episodes the woodwinds assume complete priority, in some instances being heard alone for almost thirty measures.

The beginning of the solo exposition in the Concerto in E-flat Major is especially revealing. After presenting a new theme, introductory in character, the solo part accompanies the orchestra's renewed statement of the principal theme. The piano part does not assume this theme per se; its two successive accompanimental sections merely display elaborations that perfectly blend with the bassoons and horns in the first instance and with the violin and clarinets in the second, just as the presence of the winds contributes a sense of breadth to a phrase structure underlined by particularly pianistic expression.

Passages in which octave runs are shared in both hands, an idiom generally rare in Mozart's work, appear now as a means of stressing climactic moments, for example, in the scales leading to the recapitulation of the first movement of the E-flat Major Concerto. Expressive force deriving from more intensely pianistic octave passages, such as we shall encounter again in the Concerto in D Major K. 537, occur in the final Allegro (4.11), a type of sonata rondo based on a "hunting" theme similar to that found in the Concerto in B-flat Major K. 450 and in the horn concertos also written during this period. Like the final movement of the concerto in E-flat Major K. 271, this finale makes use of a set of variations as a contrasting episode. The passage quoted in 4.11 shows certain gaps in the notation of the solo part, a not too frequent occurrence in Mozart's scores. Since this concerto, like most others, was used for his own performance, Mozart, under the pressure of time, sketched a mere outline for the solo part. In fact, only six of the seventeen concertos composed in the Vienna years were ever published during Mozart's life; the others were not prepared for engraving.

The second movements of the Concertos in E-flat Major and A Major, both

4.11. Concerto in E-flat Major K. 482, 3d movement, mm. 160–70

written in the relative minor key, are particularly expressive. The Andante in C Minor of K. 482 is marked by the color of muted strings, as was the Andantino, also in C Minor, of the Concerto in E-flat Major K. 271. Its form represents a blending of variations and rondo, the first variation developing the theme sequentially in the solo part. The *sforzati* in the closing measures of the theme, both an echo and an enrichment of the orchestral texture, generate a pianistic idiom, whose special quality is emphasized through repetition.

The Andante of the Concerto in A Major K. 488, a siciliano in the rather unusual (for Mozart) key of F-sharp Minor, stresses a dramatic contrast of register (as did the Andante of the Concerto in C Major K. 467). It is a subtle refinement of accompaniment: an expressive leap to the bass register occurs in the left-hand part. The opening motif gains harmonic momentum through the Neapolitan sixth chord, the tones of the chord being spelled out in a wide extension of the right-hand melody and variously enhanced in subsequent statements of the motif.

The lyrical quality that pervades the first movement of the Concerto in A Major finds characteristic expression in a secondary subject whose orchestral rendition suffuses and gently absorbs the broken octaves in the piano part (normally a pattern of brilliant articulation), intimately blending them with the melodic line of the violins and winds. Again, we are dealing here with a superb example of Mozart's merging of contemporary wind, string, and fortepiano sonorities. Even obviously sparkling passages entail a highly expressive handling of accompaniment and melody. Another secondary subject, appearing in a later orchestral ritornello and leading to the development, becomes the basis for an intensely polyphonic design of pianistic elaboration.

Similar is the pianistic writing in the rondo-finale, though the impression of scope and subtlety might be said to grow, given its fast tempo. The richness of part-writing that characterizes Mozart's mature work is evident throughout, yet every type of accompanimental figure remains.

The Concerto in C Minor K. 491 dates from 24 March 1786. As entered in Mozart's *Verzeichnüss*, the concerto was completed twenty-two days after the Concerto in A Major K. 488 and thus was the last of three concertos written during the period of Mozart's work on *The Marriage of Figaro* (K. 492). But its imposing style and breadth place it closer to Mozart's last concerto of 1786, the Concerto in C Major K. 503, completed in early December. With these two concertos, a decisive period in Mozart's work comes to a close: the series of twelve concertos Mozart had begun in 1784. (Two remaining concertos for piano are of a distinctly different type that will require later, separate discussion.) Significantly, Mozart appeared in only one Lenten concert in 1786 (in contrast to the nineteen public performances in March 1784 alone), and for the major part of the year 1787, he took part in no Vienna subscription concerts at all.

The Concertos K. 491 and K. 503 follow and develop the large-scale symphonic designs noted in the Concertos K. 466 and K. 467 of 1785. In a study of the sketches for the Concerto in C Minor, Alan Tyson has shown that the formal plan of the orchestral prelude presented a particular challenge.[61] Yet Mozart was also to achieve a new, expansive structure within the solo exposition, which in turn prompted a reworking of the orchestral tutti.[62] Comparisons of the types of papers Mozart used suggest that parts of some concerto sections were conceived one or two years earlier than the dates entered in Mozart's *Verzeichnüss*, which are the dates when they were completed.[63] The principal theme Mozart ultimately evolved is marked by a subtly wrought but extreme harmonic complexity: it is a modulating subject whose bold design involves an enharmonic change fully establishing the key of C minor.[64] With the Concerto in C Minor Mozart arrived at the culmination of an opulent symphonic expression evident in a fabric whose motivic development takes on unprecedented significance and whose instrumentation includes oboes and clarinets in addition to flute, bassoons, horns, trumpets, timpani, and strings.

The second of Mozart's two concertos in minor keys, this work conveys an unrelenting, tragic character as it involves both soloist and orchestra to the very closing bars of the first movement, and in contrast to the turn to the parallel major in the coda of the finale for the D Minor Concerto, the C minor tonality is maintained through the end of the finale. The first solo exposition of the Concerto in C Minor opens with a distinct theme, recitative-like in character and similar to the first solo entrance in the Concerto in D Minor. A secondary theme, fully stated only in the orchestra, gains a striking interpretation by the addition of a pianistic elaboration that moves through the gamut of the instrument's registers. The solo beginning of the first-movement development shows ever-greater refinement in the use of tone color through its exchange of registers. Set off by a two-measure interpolation in the winds, the phrases achieve a contrast greater than the appearance of the score seems to suggest (4.12). Equally arresting, finally, are the broader pianistic gestures punctuating the orchestral fabric and the simple solo rendition of the opening theme in the recapitulation, which nonetheless gains in dramatic power by widened leaps of the melodic line.

The score to the Concerto in C Minor K. 491 shows in the first movement, measures 467–70, an often-cited passage in the piano part in which Mozart used a type of shorthand to indicate, as a reminder to himself, the outline of the solo elaboration. Mozart was doubtless short of time before the first performance: the figuration established in measures 465–66 is meant to serve

4.12. Concerto in C Minor K. 491, 1st movement, mm. 283–99

as a model for the rest of the passage. As was mentioned in the case of the Concerto in D Major K. 451, in certain slow movements Mozart wrote out only what appears as a skeletal indication of his total conception, particularly when he himself appeared as soloist. But spare passages in the second movement of this C Minor Concerto hint at an instance in which the melody was meant to gain heightened expression through an unadorned and modest design, resulting, against the background of its orchestral setting, in a veritable chamber music texture. The carefully wrought and embellished figuration Mozart specifies throughout the rest of the movement unequivocally demonstrates when elaboration was intended.[65]

The theme and eight variations that make up the concluding Allegretto mark the second occasion of Mozart's use of the variation form for a finale in the piano concertos. The theme, in modest song form, rises at its phrase endings to a surprising use of the Neapolitan chord. This unusual harmonic turn—the "sixth" chord actually appears in six-four inversion by moving parts over a pedal point—receives emphasis through the variety of pianistic interpretations employed throughout the series. In the last variation (in 6/8 meter and for piano alone), it takes up an additional measure in the cadential pattern that turns into a vastly extended coda with the orchestra again joining the soloist. Two variations stand apart, those in A-flat major and in C major. Compared to the C minor variations, they seem rather like episodes, and they are marked by more modest technical demands. The total form corresponds in some degree to that of the second movement.

The first movement of the Concerto in C Major K. 503 is characterized by the most majestic proportions as well as by an enriched harmonic language. C minor, as well as C major, plays an important role in the overall tonal plan; indeed, the first of the subsidiary themes stated by the solo part turns to E-flat major (the relative key of C minor), and only with the second lyrical subject is there a decisive modulation to the dominant. From the very beginning, the grand character of the work calls forth a pianistic style echoing the symphonic sound. And yet the integrity of the solo part is maintained through pianistic brilliance. Like other compositions in C major, particularly K. 415 and K. 467, this concerto is guided by a distinct bravura; it is one of the most technically demanding of Mozart's concertos. In addition, the pianistic writing is woven into an orchestral fabric in which Mozart's motivic elaboration attains the greatest polyphonic intensity. A climactic moment in the development section places six moving parts against the solo passages of the piano (4.13).

The symphonic idiom again merges with the pianistic in the Andante, prompting extensive demands upon the soloist's technique. A remarkable transformation of roles occurs in a passage where the piano part descends a

4.13. *Concerto in C Major K. 503, 1st movement, mm. 276–79*

four-octave scale to supply the bass of the orchestral texture. Also striking is an F major episode in the last movement, in which the orchestral accompaniment is reduced to cellos and basses, followed gradually by entrances of other parts that place the blending of orchestral and pianistic sonorities into fresh perspective. The work suggests, once again, the endless possibilities and limitless scope of the Mozartean piano concerto.

SONATAS AND FANTASIES

The Sonata in D Major K. 448 (375a) for two pianos and the Sonatas in F Major K. 497 and C Major K. 521 for piano duet, written in 1781, 1786, and 1787, respectively, are related to Mozart's piano concertos in a special way. The sonatas for piano duet were written as the concerto form reached its height in Mozart's work, and they reflect the fusion of orchestra and piano within a piano duet setting that moves the genre irrevocably beyond the orbit of the *Liebhaber*. Mozart designated the parts of the autograph of the C Major Sonata K. 521 as *cembalo primo* and *cembalo secondo*, although the texture obviously involves a four-hand setting, and the intention of performance on two instruments suggests the degree of contrapuntal significance, as well as virtuosity, marking each part.

The symphonic quality of the Sonata in F major is initiated by a majestic Adagio introduction that opens the first movement (Allegro di molto). Yet the texture remains distinct from that of the duet sonatas of the 1770s. The earlier sonatas were also influenced by the orchestral idiom but the writing suggested rather an orchestral reduction; the later works are wholly pianistic, though shaped by a new symphonic ideal. A totally different sonority emerges, and passages of chordal writing are now accompanied in a pianistic style later to be identified with the generations of Beethoven and Schubert. In the second movement a contrapuntal texture, the stretto statement of a secondary theme, places two parts of the four-hand texture at opposite ends of the keyboard; similarly, extreme registers are stressed in pianistically brilliant passages, and these are juxtaposed with a tight contrapuntal texture, now written within the same register. One senses here again the influence of the late string quartets.

A definite contrast is formed by the Sonata in D Major K. 448 (375a) for two pianos, written in November 1781 for a performance by Mozart and Josephine von Auernhammer. Here we are dealing with a predominantly antiphonal type of writing for the two instruments, an approach that is often almost *buffo* in character, and the part-writing is not on the same level as that of the duet sonatas. But as a pure embodiment of the *concertante* ideal, this work is perhaps unsurpassed. Mozart wrote the *primo* part for Josephine, and the score reveals that she must have possessed an instrument that extended beyond the usual compass of the fortepiano: a phrase in the third movement reaches an f♯^{3}. Mozart must have intended to exploit the possibility of an expanded treble (the piano would have extended at least to a g^3—"white" keys defined the outer limits of the keyboard—but probably not to a c^4).

Six sonatas for piano solo were composed during the Vienna years. The Sonata in B-flat Major K. 333 (315c), begun in Linz and completed in Vienna during the fall and early winter 1783–84,[66] is the earliest work that can be dated with certainty. It had formerly been assigned, along with the Sonatas in C Major K. 330 (300h), A Major K. 331 (300i), and F Major K. 332 (300k), to the summer of 1778, the summer spent in Paris. As has been stated earlier, only the Piano Sonata in A Minor K. 310 (300d) may have been written during this period. The other three sonatas are now known to have been composed in the early 1780s, shortly before Mozart's arrival in Vienna, or during Mozart's first years in the imperial capital (in this study, they have been discussed within the context of the other works from the years of travel). The other solo sonatas include the Sonatas in C Minor K. 457, in F Major K. 533, in C Major K. 545, in B-flat Major K. 570, and D Major K. 576. Like the Sonatas in B-flat Major K. 333 (315c), the Sonata in C Minor was completed in 1784; K. 533 and K. 545 were written in 1788 and K. 570 and K. 576 in 1789. There may be another work from 1788, the Sonata in F Major (Anh. 135, K. 547a), but its authenticity seems doubtful.

A clear picture emerges. Mozart did not cultivate the sonata for solo piano extensively during the Vienna years. The first two works in the genre date from 1784. As we know, the years 1784–86 saw the composition of twelve piano concertos as well as most of the chamber music calling for piano, including the quintet, the two quartets, and the first three trios (the last three trios were written after this period, in the summer and fall of 1788). Given Mozart's achievements with the piano concerto, it is understandable that his attention did not turn toward the genre of the solo sonata until late in the decade when he completed the remaining four. The sonatas obviously represent a more personal sphere of Mozart's piano composition: they were probably written for his own use or perhaps for the purpose of instruction. Only the last sonata, the Sonata in D Major K. 576, might be the result of a particular commission. (Mozart made a trip to Berlin in 1789, at which time he may have been asked to compose the string quartets for King Friedrich Wilhelm II and keyboard music for the princess;[67] yet the composition is far from an "easy piano sonata" or "leichte Klaviersonate" as Mozart himself described it.)

It is scarcely surprising that Mozart having completed six concertos in 1784, the new symphonic concerto form should have influenced his solo sonatas. In the third movement (Allegretto grazioso) of the Sonata in B-flat Major K. 333 (315c), Mozart wrote out a *cadenza in tempo* that, like the cadenzas in the concertos, widens as well as strengthens the movement's structure and integrates further development of thematic material. The function of the cadenza is underlined by the pointed arrival at a six-four chord that sets it off and by a certain dualism of pianistic writing: a symphonic idiom in the passage leading to the cadenza contrasts markedly with the soloistic display found in the cadenza itself.

The Fantasy K. 475 and the Sonata in C Minor K. 457 were issued together as Op. 11 in 1785 by Artaria, the principal Viennese publisher of Mozart's solo sonatas and variation sets; the sonata had been completed the year before. Both works were dedicated to Thérèse von Trattner, a pupil of Mozart and the wife of an important publisher in Vienna. Though Mozart on occasion performed the works separately, their publication as a single opus implies his preference for continuity in their performance.[68] The fantasy represents Mozart's most extensive treatment of a genre that relates his writing for the piano as a solo instrument to earlier keyboard forms. Two fantasies date from 1782 and show different approaches. A Fantasy in C Minor K. 396 (385f) was begun in late summer 1782, and the autograph suggests the composition was a work for piano and violin, a movement of a sonata. However, only a few measures include the violin part; its role is slight and it seems as if the fantasy was originally conceived for piano solo. The autograph extends only to the first double bar, but an apt completion was supplied by Maximilian Stadler after Mozart's death. Indeed, the completion is so compelling in its style (especially that of the development) as to raise the argument that Stadler had at his disposal autograph material to guide his version, but if so, this has since been lost.[69]

The writing in the C Minor Fantasy K. 396 displays both the brilliant and intensely emotional qualities of improvisational keyboard forms. The latter is reflected in certain patterns ("sigh" motifs) that elaborately employ both hands, expressive passages marked by a dissonant idiom, and touches of chromaticism; also characteristic is the elaboration by trills of a dotted-rhythm pattern. Another outstanding feature is the use of scale passages in thirds for the right hand, passages possibly suggesting a conscious assimilation of the style of Clementi, but this was a gesture that Mozart would have made with some reserve. Mozart wrote to his father in 1782: "Clementi plays well, so far as execution with the right hand goes. His greatest strength lies in his passages in thirds. Apart from this, he has not a kreutzer's worth of taste or feeling— in short he is simply a *mechanicus*."[70]

The influence of C. P. E. Bach has also been proposed. This derives in part from a comparison to the style, sometimes referred to as "declamatory," of C. P. E. Bach's keyboard fantasies and in part from the fact that C. P. E. Bach's last fantasy was also scored for keyboard and violin. But the influence of C. P. E. Bach is perhaps even more strongly felt in the Fantasy in D Minor K. 397 (385b) in which, after an introductory passage of arpeggios, a type of rondo emerges, into which are interpolated cadenza-like rhapsodic passages.[71] Nonetheless, the second part of the fantasy is typically Mozartean in its turn to D major. There remains some uncertainty as to the composition's exact date; it seems to have been written in 1782, although a later date (1786–87) has been proposed. In its total impression, the Fantasy in D Minor strongly reveals Mozart's approach to this highly individual keyboard genre; yet unfortunately it remained incomplete, like the Fantasy in C Minor, and the ten measures added later, evidently by August Eberhard Müller,[72] were derived from material already present.

The pairing of fantasy and sonata in K. 475 and K. 457, however, also represents a classical counterpart to the keyboard fantasy and fugue of the baroque, but the depth of expression seems widened, too. Throughout both works the bass register gains special focus; octaves in the left hand punctuate the melody or serve as elaborations of a pedal point. In a more complex fashion, embellished octaves in the left hand are juxtaposed against a series of suspensions in a tremolo design (4.14). The exploitation of differences in register appears as a characteristic of both fantasy and sonata; it obtains perhaps its greatest intensity in the sonata, where again and again, the melody is assigned to the bass register. A particularly unusual passage places the right hand at the extreme end of the bass register in the coda to the final movement. An account by a Viennese doctor, Joseph Frank, of a piano lesson with Mozart in 1790 (one of twelve the doctor received) indicates that Mozart employed the pedal-piano— mentioned earlier in connection with the discussion of Mozart's fortepiano

4.14. Fantasy in C minor K. 475, mm. 125–26

and the Concerto in D Minor K. 466—in his performance of this piece, thus allowing additional possibilities for exploiting the bass register.[73]

As has been mentioned, equal temperament, as it is known today, was not yet pervasive in the late eighteenth century. The most typical of keyboard tuning systems involved a type of irregular temperament predicated by the adjustment of thirds (see pages 74–75, page 128 n. 35).[74] The pianistic writing of the Fantasy in C Minor, with its emphasis upon registral shifts, must be understood in terms no longer readily apparent, given the use of modern instruments. The numerous (more than ten) statements of the initial theme in distantly related keys explore the expressive possibilities of sound and nuance afforded by key and temperament. Mozart wanders as far away as the major and minor modes of B before finally arriving at the dominant, but the advent of G major, the dominant, brings with it a certain tranquility of harmonic temperament as well as "serenity" in the attainment of a harmonic—in the largest sense of the word—goal, however temporary.

The next two sonatas composed in Vienna, those in F Major K. 533 and C Major K. 545, distinctly contrast with one another. The genesis of the F Major Sonata, dated 3 January 1788, is rather complicated. Two years earlier, in 1786, Mozart had composed, as an independent piece, a Rondo in F Major K. 494, and in 1788 he wrote an Allegro and an Andante in F Major K. 533. It seems that in payment of a debt to the Viennese publisher F. A. Hoffmeister, Mozart may have been prompted to combine the two works into a sonata[75] (in 1788, Hoffmeister announced publication of a *Sonate pour le Fortepiano, ou Clavecin, Composé par W. A. Mozart*), but the adaptation required a revision of the rondo, specifically the addition of a cadenza. The expansion of the rondo now served to balance the pair of movements, which show some of Mozart's most consciously polyphonic writing for the piano. Imitative textures assume prominence throughout the first movement, and the recapitulation contains a notable passage combining the principal subject with a secondary theme. The cadenza interpolated into the rondo contains a grand stretto passage that rises from the bass to the treble register and is carried to dense five-part polyphony (4.15). Contrapuntal writing is blended with an idiom no longer typical of the sonata, one that approaches the *sonata quasi una fantasia*.

The other sonata written in 1788, the Sonata in C Major K. 545, is one of Mozart's most famous works. Mozart designated this composition *für Anfänger* and the requirements made upon pianistic capability are relatively modest, though all essential elements of keyboard technique are present. Nor is the work without contrapuntal touches; the canonic opening of the rondo has received much comment.

4.15. *Sonata in F Major K. 533, 3d movement, mm. 152–60*

Specific documents of Mozart's piano teaching, unlike those of his other pedagogical activity, are few, but one exercise survives with carefully specified fingering for each note. It suggests the type of dexterity Mozart evidently considered necessary; indeed, the changing patterns of fingering imply a technique that requires of the weak fingers (the fourth and fifth) a surprising degree of independence. It should be remembered, however, that the extremely light action of the fortepiano, with its shallow key bed and its facile hammer mechanism, offered little resistance. Thus, Mozart's exercise stressed control and thorough independence of the fingers, rather than strength per se. The exercise, published in 1982 in the *NMA* (Serie IX/27/2), dates from the second half of the 1780s and may have originated in Mozart's instruction of Johann Nepomuk Hummel, then age nine.[76]

Mozart's last two sonatas, the Sonatas in B-flat Major K. 570 and D Major K. 576, were written in February and July 1789, respectively. Though different in character, both works show a similarity in their economical use of musical ideas. In both first movements, the second theme is based upon the principal theme (a stylistic feature often associated with Haydn). And the sense of unity increases through the contrapuntal merging of themes. These sonatas are marked by a refined assimilation of polyphony that assigns melody almost equally to both hands. In the first movement of the D Major Sonata, for instance, canonic entrances of the modest, triadic theme (first at the distance of a measure and then of half a measure) form the basis of the development section. One finds everywhere in Mozart's last sonatas a certain simplification of keyboard style in which a balance is achieved through the subtle combination of pianistic and contrapuntal textures into a wholly unified expression.

VARIATIONS

Only one solo genre was cultivated by Mozart throughout the last decade: the piano variation. Ten sets of variations for piano solo and one for piano duet were written in Vienna, and they show a clear evolution of the form. Some of the sets follow the pattern of those written in Paris in 1778 (indeed, until recently, two of the Vienna sets were dated at the time of the Paris sojourn, as were some of the piano sonatas), while others undergo a development of structure comparable to that in the concerto and the sonata.

Probably one of the first compositions written after Mozart's dismissal from the service of the archbishop in June 1781 was the set of Eight Variations in F Major K. 352 (374c) on the chorus "Dieu d'amour" from A. Grétry's *Les mariages samnites*. During the period 1781–82, Mozart composed the set of Twelve Variations in C Major K. 265 (300e) on "Ah, vous dirai-je maman" and the Twelve Variations in E-flat Major K. 353 (300f) on "La belle françoise" (the French themes and the Parisian predilection for the variation form doubtless contributed to the erroneous earlier dating). The set of Six Variations in F Major K. 398 (416e) on the chorus "Salve, tu Domine" from G. Paisiello's *I filosofi immaginarii* was written in 1783, and two other sets were composed in 1784: Eight Variations in A Major K. 460 (454a) on "Come un agnello" from G. Sarti's *Fra i due litiganti il terzo gode* (the authenticity of all eight variations is questionable) and Ten Variations in G Major K. 455 on "Les hommes pieusement" ("Unser dummer Pöbel meint") from Gluck's *La rencontre imprévue*. Two sets on original themes date from 1786: Twelve Variations in B-flat Major K. 500 and Five Variations in G Major K. 501, scored for piano duet. And one variation set each marks the years 1788, 1789, and 1791: Six Variations in F Major K. 54 (547b) on an original theme, Nine Variations in D Major K. 573 on a minuet from a cello sonata by J. P. Duport,[77] and Eight Variations in F Major K. 613 on "Ein Weib ist das herrlichste Ding" from Schikaneder's play *Der dumme Gärtner*, the music for which was composed by B. Schenk and F. Gerl.

The variation sets written in the early 1780s form a special record of Mozart's improvisational gift. The impression of improvisation is particularly strong in the variations on "Salve, tu Domine" from I filosofi, in which cadenzas link the last three variations. (We know from a letter to his father that Mozart improvised a set of variations on this theme from I filosofi at a highly successful concert in 1783 for which the Emperor Joseph II was present.)[78] Evident here, too, is a freer handling of the variation form, for at times the construction of the variations no longer corresponds strictly to the formal design of the theme. Sustained trills, a favorite Mozartean expression of pianistic brilliance, are now transferred to the bass register, and a rhapsodic expression characterizes the last variation through figurations suggestive of Beethoven's pianistic writing and culminating in a cadenza.

The variations on "Unser dummer Pöbel meint," written in 1784, reflect the influence of Mozart's concertos through passages exploring the extreme ranges of the keyboard as well as through various cadenzas. In addition, a virtuoso quality evident in certain keyboard figurations suggests the need to balance an orchestral force. The bravura of the eighth variation seems to transform the theme completely, and the overall expansiveness of the last three variations approaches the symphonic variation style; at the same time, the increasing scope of the final Allegro variation produces a sense of classical sonata design.

Abert has observed that the pianistic writing in the Variations in B-flat Major K. 500 on an original theme hints at the stylistic influence of Clementi. He cites a triplet figuration (in the first two variations), a distinctive accompanimental bass (fourth variation), and chordal writing for both hands in the treble register (variation eight) as typical of Clementi's pianistic style.[79] This is especially intriguing given the background of the famous contest between Mozart and Clementi in December 1781. It is known that the two composers improvised, both together and separately, and that Mozart was impressed with Clementi's facility for passages in double-thirds, an innovation of piano technique attributed to him.[80] The publication of a number of Clementi's compositions in the 1780s may have contributed to a pointed assimilation of this stylistic trait.[81]

Mozart wrote his last variation set in March 1791. The Eight Variations in F Major K. 613 on "Ein Weib ist das herrlichste Ding" offer a somewhat different structural organization arising from the pianistic writing itself. The theme consists of three sections instead of the usual two; and the first section is varied throughout in a manner that sets it apart from the other sections and their respective variations (Mozart's treatment suggests that the first eight bars of the song might have served as an instrumental introduction). A type of dual variation pattern emerges that places in relief various keyboard figurations while additionally presenting the contrast of major and minor modes. The Adagio variation, traditionally florid, is particularly elaborate, and a looser formal outline produces a more dramatic transformation of the theme. Still more striking is the concluding Allegro: the introductory phrase of the theme does not appear until the end, as a coda, and the variation itself evolves into a kind of symphonic fantasy involving a surprising modulation to D-flat major.[82]

The piano variation form remained one of the most individual of Mozart's expressions. Nonetheless, it reflects his work in other genres, as well as the entire stylistic development of his last ten years. A wide variety of idioms marks its pianistic style and runs the gamut from an intimate chamber music character to the most elaborate concert bravura; it points, finally, to the expanded variation cycles of later generations and to new pianistic forms.

5

The Last Phase

*

A few works need to be separated from those discussed in the preceding chapter, for they form a bridge to the brief but momentous final chapter of the
composer's life in the early 1790s. Having led the form of the symphonic
concerto to a supreme point in the Concerto in C Major K. 503, Mozart returned to the genre a little more than a year later, but with an altogether different conception. The Concerto in D Major K. 537, to which "we may quite
properly apply the term 'hors d'oeuvre,' " meaning "apart from the main
body of works,"[1] is an ingratiating work of modest dimensions that might be
linked to Mozart's last pieces for solo piano, intimate in character and scale,
rather than to his piano concertos of the period.

A novel use of pianistic virtuosity is found in this concerto, known as the
Coronation Concerto because Mozart performed the work in Frankfurt during
the festivities surrounding the accession of Leopold II to the Imperial throne.
Playful virtuosity now becomes an integral part of the texture, and it is this
feature, a certain joy in the virtuoso element, that distinguishes this concerto
and places it, in a sense, at the head of the early nineteenth-century concerto
repertoire, "closest to the early or proto-Romantic style of Hummel and Weber."[2] (It was to remain one of Mozart's most popular piano concertos during
the nineteenth century.) A bright use of keyboard figuration marks the first
and third movements. The resulting passagework produces a subtle stretching
of form, evading cadences. The balance shifts toward virtuosity of the solo
part, and the total impression that emerges is that of a different interpretation
of the concerto genre. The virtuoso element itself now plays a decisive role in
the reoriented total structure, one in which the greater emphasis is on melodic
rather than harmonic structure—a style characteristic of the early nineteenth-
century concerto of Hummel, Weber, Beethoven, and Chopin. Indeed, this
aspect of K. 537 bears a striking resemblance to passages in Beethoven's Concerto in C Major Op. 15.[3] Mozart's *Coronation* Concerto was first published in

1794 by Johann André, so it is possible that Beethoven became familiar with the work after his permanent move to the Imperial capital in 1792.

An element similar to this type of virtuosity appears in a repertory that requires mention at this point, the cadenzas for piano concertos that are grouped in the Köchel Verzeichnis under the collective number K. 624 (626aI and II, next to the listing of the Requiem K. 626). Included in this large collection are cadenzas for the works of other composers as well as for Mozart's own concerto arrangements and concertos. We know now that some of the extant cadenzas were not integrated originally but were composed for certain performances;[4] consequently, there is often a considerable difference in the dates of concerto and cadenza. That circumstance enables us to witness the evolution of the Mozartean cadenza as it gradually becomes an integral part of the composition: it assumes the individual character of each work and becomes an innate element of the concerto form.[5] This process is so complete that the interpenetration must be understood both ways. The virtuosity of the cadenza becomes an element germane to the concerto, and its assimilation of thematic development so transforms the cadenza that it becomes inseparable from the larger work, a blending inherited by Beethoven that led to the perfected cadenza form in his last piano concerto.

The fact that there was no opportunity for publication of the *Coronation Concerto* during Mozart's life may explain its incomplete form. In the context of the present discussion, it is especially regrettable that Mozart wrote out no cadenzas for this work. In fact, the autograph of this concerto again contains extensive sections where the staff for the left hand is blank, and in other sections, Mozart's notations for the right hand present only an outline rather than the complete realization of passage work.[6]

The totally contrasting element of the concerto that signals a new stylistic feature of Mozart's late works is a simplicity of expression, a certain naïveté (as pronounced as that of the virtuosity in the first and third movements) that marks the pianistic style of the Larghetto. This folk-like character, although rare, appears also in other instrumental works (such as the fourth and sixth movements of the Divertimento in E-flat Major K. 563 for string trio), but it becomes most explicit in the form of song (e.g., Papageno's "Der Vogelfänger ich bin ja" and "Sehnsucht nach dem Frühlinge" K. 596). The nature of the concerto's second movement is determined by this "consciously" simple style (Charles Rosen uses the term *faux-naïf*),[7] which became an aspect of the nineteenth-century *Lied*. The Larghetto offers typically Mozartean pianistic writing, but its aim is not easy to convey: the challenge is now to realize the quality of song through the medium of the piano (5.1).

5.1. Concerto in D Major K. 537, 2d movement, mm. 1–4

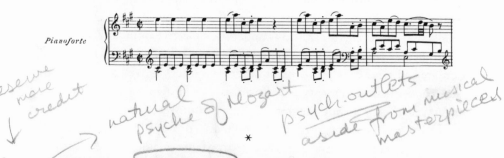

Pianoforte

deserve more credit

natural psyche of Mozart

psych. outlets aside from musical masterpieces

✳

Another element of Romantic art becomes significant in Mozart's last solo keyboard works. Having exhausted the possibilities of the large structural frame of the piano sonata and the expansive improvisatory genres of fantasy and variation, his solo writing now suggests a return to the earliest forms of isolated dance or sonata movements, though fundamentally changed in character. These compositions date from the late 1780s, and each commands such a highly personal, subjective tone that they may be regarded as antecedents of the nineteenth-century "character" piece. The group includes the Rondo in A Minor K. 511, composed in 1787; the Adagio in B Minor K. 540, written in 1788; the Gigue in G Major K. 574, composed in 1789; and the Minuet in D Major K. 335 (594a; KV6: 576b), dating from 1789 or 1790.

Mozart referred to the Rondo in A Minor K. 511 as *Ein Rondo für das klavier allein* when entering it in his catalog of works. The special sense of the instrument's isolation in its solo role seems to be heightened by the sensitive blending of varieties of touch and the dynamic expression with which they are underlined (5.2). Nonetheless, the elaboration of the theme approaches symphonic dimensions while never abandoning a truly pianistic idiom.

An immediacy of tragic tone marks the character of these last piano pieces. Small melodic and rhythmic motifs, seemingly concentrated upon emotion, grow to new proportions, and the *Empfindsamkeit* of the late eighteenth-century keyboard literature sinks into the past. The variation structure within the pattern of the rondo is stressed by the deliberate design of a section in the corresponding major, as it is in the harmonic compass, and the blending of rondo and variations is so perfect that the listener is scarcely aware of the instrumental virtuosity with which it is accomplished. Yet as early as the first episode, we encounter passages that suggest Chopin's pianistic style (5.3). Nor is the contrapuntal finesse obtrusive that leads, in the last varied suggestions of the theme, to an augmentation in the middle part (5.4).

The Rondo in A Minor forms a particularly notable contrast to another

Rondo in a

①

✳ *vehicle of musical affective expression + intellectual intricacy (cntpt.)*

5.2. *Rondo in A Minor K. 511, mm. 1–12*

5.3. *Rondo in A Minor K. 511, mm. 58–61*

isolated work, the Rondo in D Major K. 485 (written in 1786). The latter, based on a well-known theme that goes back to J. C. Bach, suggests the spirit of the *Sonate für Anfänger* rather than that of the last solo works. It was apparently intended for an aristocratic amateur,[8] and its typically *galant* elegance implies a commissioned work rather than a work of purely personal expression. Yet as in the sonata, the pianistic simplicity is deceiving, and it is paired

5.4. Rondo in A Minor K. 511, mm. 176–82

with great virtuosity of composition. While a rondo in name and spirit, the work is in its design a classical example of sonata form—clearly designated as a sonata movement, on the other hand, is an Allegro in G Minor K. 312 (590d), which dates from 1789 or 1790, but this piece represents a fragment that breaks off at the end of the exposition.[9]

✳ In the case of the B Minor Adagio K. 540, one might again raise the question (and perhaps more justifiably than for the two rondos mentioned above) whether we are concerned with a fragment from an unfinished sonata. But Mozart's title *Ein Adagio für das klavier allein in H moll* points again to the nature of a new genre. It is "one of the most perfect, most deeply felt and most despairing of all his works."[10]

A tone of utter seriousness, reminiscent of the G Minor String Quintet K. 516, is set with the entry of a single voice, the answering *sforzando* chord, and the subsequent octave contours of the melody (5.5). The declamatory exchange of thematic statements in high and low registers underlines an expression of profundity that now dominates the musical fabric. Out of the elaboration of each idea arises a style that is at once contrapuntal and totally

5.5. *Adagio in B Minor K. 540, mm. 1–6*

characteristic of the expression of the early nineteenth century. Also typical of early nineteenth-century idiom is the *Lied*-like distribution of melody and accompaniment.

The pianistic idioms—sudden juxtapositions of dynamics, broken octave passages, motivic accents placed in widely separated registers through hand crossing—convey melancholy throughout. Especially interesting is the middle section, with its broad harmonic scope but economic means of development. A "Brahmsian" duplet-triplet figure on the Neapolitan sixth-chord leads to the cadence ending the recapitulation (5.6). Again we are reminded of the last string quintets. And the spirit of the C Major Quintet K. 515, a serenity beyond all melancholy, transfigures the coda with its shift to B major and a final pianistic gesture of oscillating chord motion in both hands.

The remaining two pieces seem to venture into further regions. The Gigue in G Major K. 574 and the Minuet in D Major K. 355 (594a; KV6: 576b) are without parallel in Mozart's work. The gigue was written during Mozart's visit to Leipzig in May 1789; it was entered into an album of the court organist Karl Immanuel Engel. The warm dedication to Engel that Mozart added bears

5.6. Adagio in B Minor K. 540, mm. 48–49

the date 16 May, and the circumstances of Mozart's travel dismiss any later dating, though Mozart himself did not include the piece in his own catalog until 17 May.[11] Mozart had stopped in Leipzig twice. During his initial visit in April, he improvised on the organ of St. Thomas's Church before the Cantor, Johann Friedrich Doles, a pupil of J. S. Bach, and the organist Karl Friedrich Görner, whose father, Johann Gottlieb Görner, had held the post of organist during J. S. Bach's cantorate. During these days, or possibly when Mozart returned in May, he heard a performance of Bach's motet *Singet dem Herrn ein neues Lied* for double chorus, and this first encounter with Bach's choral polyphony made the deep impression upon Mozart that has been recorded by one of the St. Thomas alumni.[12] It has been suggested that, as a result of this experience, the gigue was a gesture in homage to Bach. But there is a stronger association with the work of Handel: Mozart's work bears an undeniable resemblance to the gigue from Handel's Suite in F Minor, the eighth in the collection issued in 1720.[13]

Some of Mozart's most concentratedly contrapuntal writing for keyboard occurs within the thirty-eight measures of this gigue. The work, beginning as a three-part fugue on a chromatic and melodically complex theme (the subject involves ten of the twelve tones of the chromatic scale), turns at the double bar to fugal treatment of the inverted theme similar to the manner of the typical Baroque keyboard gigue. But here the *inversus* forms merely the answer to the *rectus,* so that we are now dealing instead with the counterfugue structure of the Renaissance.

The technical difficulty for the performer is in the integrity of polyphonic structure: achieving clear articulation of voices within a complicated contrapuntal fabric. The work's playful character changes in the reiterated pedal points into a heroic tone that begins to suffuse the whole structure with a remarkable blending of lightness and weight (5.7).

The resurgence of a contrapuntal style that links Mozart's writing to the late Baroque may have been influenced by his thorough study of Fux's *Gradus*

5.7. Gigue in G Major K. 574, mm. 1–12, 24–38

ad Parnassum, which is documented in the instruction he gave some of his most gifted students in the later 1780s.[14] Polyphony is so totally absorbed in Mozart's late style that Wolfgang Plath, in his edition of what is probably Mozart's last solo work for piano, suggests that its keyboard scoring (for which no autograph has survived) may represent a transcribed string quartet texture.[15] It is a minuet, like Mozart's very first preserved work. But its densely woven chromatic pathos makes it "the most mournful of all minuets."[16] The dating of the Minuet in D Major K. 355 (594a; KV6: 576b), as the various Köchel numbers indicate, has been subjected to frequent reexamination. The latest research places the work in either 1789 or 1790.[17] The stylized dance now assumes the most abstract quality, seeming to move beyond the limits of its genre yet always finding the most convincing expression in the piano.

The opening and closing measures of the first section might be described as truly pianistic. The contrapuntal development of the closing motif is immediately subjected to diminution with a figure that leads to an extended passage in octaves. The resulting numerous inversion and stretto formations of the theme are blended with natural ease into the intimate, song-like nature of the *Phantasiestück*. In this small work, we have reached a point of ultimate expression in Mozart's keyboard style (5.8).

✳

It is curiously appropriate that the final keyboard work Mozart wrote should have been a concerto, as was his last instrumental composition, the clarinet concerto. The Piano Concerto in B-flat Major K. 595 is dated 5 January 1791, and it was performed by Mozart himself on 4 March in his last public performance, a concert organized by the clarinetist Josef Bähr and given at the great hall of the inn of the court caterer Ignaz Jahn. The B-flat Major Concerto and the Concerto in A Major K. 622 for clarinet share a certain intimate quality that distinguishes them from the series of concertos of the late 1780s. They also stand apart from the Concerto in D Major K. 537, in which a new ideal of virtuosity had been introduced. The Concerto in B-flat Major followed the three last symphonies, completed during the summer of 1788. It is significant that Mozart's symphonic style, which had been profoundly influenced through the vehicle of the piano concerto as early as the Concerto in E-flat Major K. 271[18] and which had achieved its purest expression in these three symphonies, emerges once more in a concerto but this time as something rather different. The symphonic concerto is transformed, and the sense that its orchestral style is refined to a chamber music style serves only partly as an explanation. One finds an analogously complicated and subtle development

5.8. Minuet in D Major K. 355 (594; KV6: 576b), mm. 17–40

in the last six masses of Haydn, written over the period 1796–1802, in which the composer moves beyond the achievement of his symphonies, pursuing a new ideal through a perfected medium.[19] We are reminded of Mozart having singled out his piano quintet with wind instruments as his best work. The clarinet trio and eventually the clarinet concerto are linked to the particular polyphonic style that emerged with this quintet score, and the emphasis upon the element of the woodwind sound returns with the B-flat Major Concerto. But it compares to Mozart's other piano concertos as the last single pieces compare to the earlier solo works.

The source situation is involved, and only by recourse to material from private collections of Toscanini, Rudolf Serkin, and Paul Badura-Skoda were the editors of the *NMA* able to present a reliable text.[20] Characteristic of editorial problems that almost defy solution is the example (quoted in the preface and critical report of the *NMA*) of a practically illegible correction Mozart entered in the autograph in what the editor refers to as "Puccini fifths,"[21] which arise through an orchestral octave doubling. But in its melodic doubling of the sonorities for flute, violin, and piano, the passage is also characteristic of a last phase in Mozart's instrumentation and a final blend of intimacy and grandeur. "It was not in the Requiem that he said his last word . . . but in this work, which belongs to a species in which he also said his greatest."[22]

Perhaps the most significant detail to be mentioned in connection with the B-flat Major Concerto is the theme of its third movement, because immediately after the composition of the concerto, Mozart used this theme for one of his most famous songs, "Sehnsucht nach dem Frühlinge" K. 596. Having reached the end of Mozart's pianistic work, we witness an afterglow of the pianistic medium in his last songs.

The piano had assumed the dominant role it was to take in the Romantic *Lied* in such works as "Das Veilchen" K. 476, "Das Lied der Trennung" K. 519, "Als Luise die Briefe" K. 520, "Abendempfindung" K. 523, "An Chloe" K. 524, and "Das Traumbild" K. 530. Even the last example of the genre, the cantata "Die ihr des unermesslichen Weltalls" K. 619, is written for voice and piano. The song thus becomes the most eloquent harbinger of both the idiomatic lyricism and simplicity (K. 598 is entitled "Das Kinderspiel") and of the fully emancipated role the piano attained in Mozart's work.

*

The pianistic genres play an encompassing role in Mozart's lifework, and while the development of his style emerges with equal clarity in all of them, two stand out. It is Mozart the polyphonist and the symphonist who involved the instrument in new phases that were to have the greatest significance: classic chamber music and the classic concerto. In a way, the classic keyboard sonata stands before us as early as 1742 with the issue of C. P. E. Bach's *Prussian Sonatas*. While Mozart cultivated the genre through the popular accompanied form in sonatas written during his childhood, the role of violin accompaniment disappeared and the classical sonata emerged fully in Mozart's solo sonatas for piano and the ensemble sonatas for piano and violin composed in the 1770s. And commensurate with the evolution of form in Mozart's work was the formation of a genuine pianistic style. The continued development of the genre, while reflecting Mozart's work in other media, moved the sonata to a point at which it could embrace an instrumental form of great contrapuntal involvement as well as the seemingly simple "work for beginners."

In the number and variety of his solo pieces, Mozart also assumed the forms current at the time, but he transformed them to such a degree that his pianistic style seems to transcend his own era. The fantasy and variation forms, bequests of Baroque keyboard art, underwent in Mozart's work a similar development. The influence of the sonata principle explains the achievement only to a degree: the parallel evolution of the pianistic idiom unequivocally contributed to their stature, linking them to the larger forms of the nineteenth century.

In the sphere of chamber music, however, Mozart produced an entirely new literature. While the ensemble sonata and the trio for piano and strings once again developed out of Baroque models, the duo and trio sonatas for obbligato instruments and continuo, the increased demands for music addressed to the amateur and the development of the keyboard instrument decisively affected the cultivation of a new chamber music repertoire in the later eighteenth century. And Mozart's contributions placed the genre on a level that, though representing the art of the connoisseur, went far beyond it. It is not surprising that the genre most closely associated with the connoisseur, the string quartet, uniquely influenced Mozart's work. The string quartets dedicated to Haydn ushered in the era of Mozart's final achievements in chamber music. Their distinguishing feature, classical polyphony, gained greatest expression not only in the string quartet and quintet but equally in Mozart's chamber music with piano. And the very embodiment of Mozart's chamber music style is his creation of the classical ensemble employing woodwinds and piano.

In fact the writing for woodwinds, its realization through polyphony, in the hands of Mozart established to a great extent the classical concerto as a symphonic genre. The concerto occupied Mozart throughout his life, both as a personal vehicle for performance and as the medium through which he expressed most fully his symphonic imagination. Inasmuch as Mozart essentially initiated, developed, and perfected the classical concerto, he achieved a pianistic form of consummate perfection that opened the way toward the literature of a new century. It is difficult to believe that the enormous arch from rococo to Romanticism could be drawn in the span of such a short creative life. Yet nowhere is the scope of Mozart's work more evident than in his keyboard writing and in the keyboard genres that owe their rise to him.

Notes

Bibliography

Indexes

Notes

The abbreviation *MJb* refers to the *Mozart Jahrbuch* (Salzburg, 1950–), a yearly publication issued by the Internationale Stiftung Mozarteum, and the abbreviation *NMA* refers to *Wolfgang Amadeus Mozart: Neue Ausgabe sämtlicher Werke* (Kassel: Bärenreiter, 1956–91) the critical edition of Mozart's works.

PREFACE

1. Cf. Christoph Wolff, "New Research on Bach's *Musical Offering*," *Musical Quarterly* 57 (July 1971): 401–3.

2. See Ludwig Finscher, "Bach und die Wiener Klassik," *Bach-Tage, Vorträge 1975* (Berlin: published with the program book Bach-Tage 1977), 15.

1. THE YOUNG KEYBOARD VIRTUOSO

1. Eric Blom, *The Romance of the Piano* (London: G. T. Foulis, 1928; New York: Da Capo Press, 1969), 111–12.

2. Théodore de Wyzewa and Georges de Saint-Foix, *W.-A. Mozart, sa vie et son oeuvre de l'enfance a la pleine maturité* (Paris: Desclée de Brouwer et cie, 1936), 1: 41–45.

3. Eduard Reeser, Preface, *NMA*, Serie VIII, *Kammermusik*, Werkgruppe 23: *Sonaten und Variationen für Klavier und Violine*, Band 1 (Kassel: Bärenreiter, 1964), vii–x.

4. Reeser, Preface, *NMA*, Serie VIII/23/1, vii–x.

5. In a letter dated London, 3 Dec. 1764. Emily Anderson, *The Letters of Mozart and His Family*, 3d edition corrected by Stanley Sadie and Fiona Smart, after 2d edition prepared by A. Hyatt King and Monica Carolan (New York: Norton, 1985), 53.

6. Reeser, Preface, *NMA*, Serie VIII/23/1, vii–x.

7. In a letter dated Paris, 1 Feb. 1764, in Anderson, 37.

8. The sources for these arrangements were first mentioned by Wyzewa and Saint-Foix, 1:87. They have been recently considered in detail by Eduard Reeser, Preface, *NMA*, Serie X, *Supplement*, Werkgruppe 28: *Bearbeitungen, Ergänzungen und Übertragungen fremder Werke*, Abteilung 2: *Bearbeitungen von Werken verschiedener Komponisten, Klavierkonzerte und Kadenzen* (Kassel: Bärenreiter, 1964), x–xi.

9. Reeser, Preface, *NMA*, Serie X/28/2, ix.

10. F. E. Kirby, *A Short History of Keyboard Music* (New York: Free Press, 1966), 185.

11. Reeser, Preface, *NMA*, Serie X/28/2, xi–xii.

12. Alfred Einstein, *Mozart, His Character, His Work,* trans. Arthur Mendel and Nathan Broder (London: Oxford University Press, 1945), 119.

13. In a letter dated St. Germain, 27 Aug. 1778, in Anderson, 606.

14. Melchior von Grimm, "Correspondance Littéraire," Paris, 15 July 1776, in Otto Erich Deutsch, *Mozart, A Documentary Biography,* trans. Eric Blom, Peter Branscombe, and Jeremy Noble (London: Adam and Charles Black, 1965), 57.

15. Daines Barrington, Report on Mozart, handed to the Royal Society, London, 28 Sept. 1769, read before the Learned Society, 15 Feb. 1770, in Deutsch, 98–99. Barrington's account is concerned with Mozart's visit to London during the summer of 1765.

16. Charles Sanford Terry, *John Christian Bach* (London: Oxford University Press, 1929), 80. See also *The New Grove Dictionary of Music and Musicians,* s.v. "Johann Christian Bach" by Ernest Warburton, 1: 865–76; and Heinz Gärtner, *Johann Christian Bach, Mozarts Freund und Lehrmeister* (Munich: Nymphenberger, F. A. Herbig Verlagsbuchhandlung GmbH, 1989).

17. In a letter dated London, 28 May 1764, in Anderson, 47.

18. Wolfgang Plath and Wolfgang Rehm, Preface, *NMA,* Serie VIII, *Kammermusik,* Werkgruppe 22: Abteilung 2: *Klaviertrios* (Kassel: Bärenreiter, 1966), vii–x.

19. Wolfgang Plath, Preface, *NMA,* Serie IX, *Klaviermusik,* Werkgruppe 27: *Klavierstücke,* Band 1: *Die Notenbücher* (Kassel: Bärenreiter, 1982). See also Neal Zaslaw, "Leopold Mozart's List of His Son's Work," in *Music of the Classical Period: Essays in Honor of Barry S. Brook,* ed. Allan Atlas (New York: Pendragon Press, 1985), 323–58; and Neal Zaslaw, *Mozart's Symphonies: Context, Performance Practice, Reception* (New York: Oxford University Press, 1989), 18–29.

20. Wolfgang Plath, "Beiträge zur Mozart-Autographie I: Die Handschrift Leopold Mozarts," *MJb 1960–61,* 82–117; Wolfgang Plath, "Leopold Mozarts Notenbuch für Wolfgang (1762)—eine Fälschung?," *MJb 1971–72,* 337–41.

21. Walter Gerstenberg, Preface, *NMA,* Serie X, *Supplement,* Werkgruppe 28: *Bearbeitungen, Ergänzungen und Übertragungen fremder Werke,* Abteilung 2: *Bearbeitungen von Werken verschiedener Komponisten, Klavierkonzerte und Kadenzen* (Kassel: Bärenreiter, 1964), xvii–xviii.

22. Reeser, Preface, *NMA,* Serie X/28/2, xii.

23. Gerstenberg, Preface, *NMA,* Serie X/28/2, xii.

24. Christopher Hogwood, Introduction, *J. C. Bach: Twelve Keyboard Sonatas (Opera V)* ([London]: Oxford University Press, 1973); facsimile ed. of "Six Sonatas for the Piano Forte or Harpsichord composed by John Christian Bach," Opera 5 (London: Welcher, ca. 1768).

25. See, however, Eva Badura-Skoda, "Prolegomena to a History of the Viennese Fortepiano," *Israel Studies in Musicology* 2 (1980): 77–99. See also Eva Badura-Skoda, "Zur Frühgeschichte des Hammerklaviers," *Florilegium Musicologium: Festschrift Hellmut Federhofer* (Tutzing: Hans Schneider Verlag, 1988).

26. *The New Grove Dictionary of Music and Musicians,* s.v. "Domenico Alberti" by Michael Talbot, 1: 211.

27. von Grimm, "Correspondance Littéraire," Paris, 1 Dec. 1763, in Deutsch, 26.

28. Program of Mozart's concert at the Teatro Scientifico, Mantua, 16 Jan. 1770, in Deutsch, 106–7.

29. *Gazetta di Mantova,* 19 Jan. 1770, in Deutsch, 107.

2. MOZART AND THE TRANSFORMATION OF KEYBOARD PRACTICE

1. Cf. Hanns Dennerlein, "Mozarts europäische Orgelerfahrung," *MJb 1978–79,* 269.

2. In a letter dated London, 28 May 1764, in Anderson, 47.

3. In a letter dated Augsburg, 24 Oct. 1777, in Anderson, 339.

4. Anderson, 340.

5. Dennerlein, "Mozarts europäische Orgelerfahrung," 274–275.

6. Dennerlein, "Mozarts europäische Orgelerfahrung," 275.

7. Cf. Georg Nikolaus von Nissen, *Biographie W. A. Mozarts* (Leipzig, 1828; facsimile ed., Hildesheim: Georg Olms Verlagsbuchhandlung, 1964), 566.

8. Third movement, measure 21.

9. Paul Henry Lang, *Music in Western Civilization* (New York: Norton, 1941), 649.

10. Einstein, *Mozart,* 237.

11. Nathan Broder, "Mozart and the 'Clavier,' " in *The Creative World of Mozart,* ed. Paul Henry Lang (New York: Norton, 1964), 82–85.

12. *The Grove Dictionary of Musical Instruments,* s.v. "Pianoforte," 3: 71–78.

13. See William S. Newman, "Beethoven's Pianos Versus His Piano Ideals," *Journal of the American Musicological Society* 29 (Fall 1970): 484–504; William S. Newman, *Beethoven on Beethoven: Playing His Piano His Way* (New York: Norton, 1988).

14. David Wainwright, *Broadwood, By Appointment* (London: Quiller Press, 1982), 36–38.

15. Wainwright, 35–36.

16. Christian Friedrich David Schubart, *Deutsche Chronik,* Augsburg, 27 Apr. 1775, in Deutsch, 153.

17. In a letter dated Augsburg, 17 Oct. 1777, in Anderson, 328–29.

18. Broder, 78.

19. Johann Friedrich Agricola, "Bach on Silbermann's Pianofortes," in *The Bach Reader,* ed. Hans T. David and Arthur Mendel (New York: Norton, 1966), 259.

20. Wolff, "New Research," 399–403; cf. the Preface, p. x.

21. Wolff, "New Research," 403.

22. Cf. F. E. Kirby, *A Short History of Keyboard Music* (New York: Free Press, 1966), 145.

23. Johann Georg Sulzer, *"Allgemeine Theorie der schönen Künste,"* 2nd edn., 1792–94 in *Music and Aesthetics in the Eighteenth and Early-Nineteenth Centuries,* ed. James Day and Peter le Huray (Cambridge: Cambridge University Press, 1981), 124–27.

24. Ulrich Rück, "Mozarts Hammerflügel erbaute Anton Walter, Wien," *MJb 1955,* 246–62. See also Sandra P. Rosenblum, *Performance Practices in Classic Piano Music* (Bloomington: Indiana University Press, 1988), 31–51.

25. Lang, 723.

26. Broder, 78.

27. "Specificatio of the Estate Left by the Late Mr. Johann Sebastian Bach Formerly Cantor at the Thomas-Schule in Leipzig, Departed in God July 28, 1750, " in David and Mendel, 197.

28. Carl Philipp Emanuel Bach, *Essay on the True Art of Playing Keyboard Instruments,* trans. and ed. William J. Mitchell (New York: Norton, 1949); Daniel Gottlob Türk, *Kla-*

vierschule (Leipzig & Halle, 1789; facsimile ed. Erwin R. Jacobi, Kassel: Bärenreiter, 1967); see also Raymond H. Haggh, *School of Clavier Playing, or, Instructions in Playing the Clavier for Teachers and Students by Daniel Gottlob Türk,* trans. with notes by Raymond H. Haggh (Lincoln: University of Nebraska Press, 1982).

29. Bach, 172, 36.

30. Türk, 7, 1.

31. Türk, ornamentation, 200–331; fingering, 129–99; basic elements, 33–129; performance, 332–76.

32. Bach, 41–78.

33. Türk, 376–408.

34. See William J. Mitchell, Introduction, *Essay on the True Art of Playing Keyboard Instruments,* by Carl Philipp Emanuel Bach, trans. and ed. William J. Mitchell (New York: Norton, 1949), 13–14.

3. THE LAST YEARS OF TRAVEL

1. Jens Peter Larsen, "The Symphonies," in *The Mozart Companion,* ed. H. C. Robbins Landon and Donald Mitchell (New York: Norton, 1969), 156–58.

2. Larsen, "The Symponies," 159–63.

3. Larsen, "The Symphonies," 169–70. Cf., however, the detailed discussion of the symphonies of this period in Zaslaw, *Mozart's Symphonies.*

4. Einstein, *Mozart,* 171.

5. Deutsch, 166, 168.

6. "[Mozart] favoured the company by performing fantasies and capriccios on the pianoforte. His feeling, the rapidity of his fingers, the great execution and strength of his left hand, particularly, and the apparent inspiration of his modulations, astounded me" (Michael Kelly, *Reminiscences of Michael Kelly* [London, 1826; London: Oxford University Press, 1975], 112).

7. *The New Grove Dictionary of Music and Musicians,* s.v. "Wolfgang Amadeus Mozart" by Stanley Sadie, 12: 693–93; Wolfgang Plath, "Beiträge zur Mozart-Autographie II: Schriftchronologie 1770–1780," *MJb* 1976–77, 153–67; Wolfgang Plath, "Zur Datierung der Klaviersonaten KV 279–284," *Acta Mozartiana* 21 (Aug. 1974): 26–30.

8. In a letter dated Mannheim, 4 Feb. 1778, in Anderson, 459–63.

9. *The New Grove Dictionary of Music and Musicians,* s.v. "Joseph Haydn" by Jens Peter Larsen, 8: 353.

10. A. Peter Brown, *Joseph Haydn's Keyboard Music, Sources and Style* (Bloomington: Indiana University Press, 1986), 302.

11. Wyzewa and Saint-Foix, 2: 186–93.

12. Eva Badura-Skoda and Paul Badura-Skoda, *Interpreting Mozart on the Keyboard,* trans. Leo Black (New York: St. Martin's, 1962), 63–64. See also Ewald Zimmermann, "Das Mozart-Preisausschreiben der Gesellschaft für Musikforschung," in *Festschrift Joseph Schmidt-Görg,* ed. Dagmar Weise (Bonn: Beethovenhaus Verlag, 1957), 400–408; Paul Mies, "Die Artikulationszeichen Strich und Punkt bei Wolfgang Amadeus Mozart," *Die Musikforschung* 11 (1958): 428–55.

13. Eva Badura-Skoda and Paul Badura-Skoda, *Interpreting Mozart*, 65–68. See, however, Robert Daniel Riggs, "Articulation in Mozart's and Beethoven's Sonatas for Piano and Violin: Source-Critical and Analytic Studies" (Ph.D. diss., Harvard University, 1987).

14. Eva Badura-Skoda and Paul Badura-Skoda, *Interpreting Mozart*, 53–63. For a thorough discussion of the issues related to articulation and touch, see also Rosenblum, 149–89.

15. Eugene K. Wolf, "On the Origins of the Mannheim Symphonic Style," in *Studies in Musicology in Honor of Otto E. Albrecht,* ed. John Walter Hill (Kassel: Bärenreiter, 1980), 197–239; *The New Grove Dictionary of Music and Musicians*, s.v. "Mannheim Style" by Eugene K. Wolf, 11: 629–30.

16. In a letter dated Mannheim, 11 Dec. 1777, in Anderson, 416–18.

17. In a letter dated Mannheim, 6 Dec. 1777, in Anderson, 407–8.

18. In a letter dated Mannheim, 14 Nov. 1777, in Anderson, 373–75.

19. In a letter dated Mannheim, 28 Dec. 1777, in Anderson, 436.

20. In a letter dated Paris, 27 July 1778, from von Grimm to Leopold Mozart, in Deutsch, 177.

21. Despite Mozart's claims, it seems that only one symphony was actually written in Paris for the *Concert spirituel*. See Neal Zaslaw, "Mozart's Paris Symphonies," *Musical Times* 119 (1978): 753–57. See also Zaslaw, *Mozart's Symphonies*, 306–34.

22. Giorgio Pestelli, *The Age of Mozart and Beethoven*, trans. Eric Cross (Cambridge: Cambridge University Press, 1984), 27–29.

23. *The New Grove Dictionary of Music and Musicians*, s.v. "Johann Schobert" by Herbert C. Turrentine, 16: 697.

24. Herbert C. Turrentine, "Johann Schobert and French Clavier Music from 1700 to the Revolution" (Ph.D. diss., University of Iowa, 1962), 1: 313–15.

25. In a letter dated Munich, 6 Oct. 1777, in Anderson, 299–301.

26. In a letter dated Mannheim, 14 Feb. 1778, in Anderson, 481–82.

27. Einstein, *Mozart*, 254.

28. Türk, 191–92.

29. Einstein has noted the coincidence of two *opera* designated 1 and two *opera* designated 2, all of them collections of sonatas for piano and violin that were published during Mozart's life. The first pair, products of Mozart's childhood, were issued at Paris in 1764; Op. 1 was dedicated to the Princesse Victoire, Op. 2 to the Comtesse de Tessé. The second pair represent mature expressions of the genre. The later Op. 1 was issued at Paris in 1778 and dedicated to Maria Elisabeth, wife of the Elector of the Palatinate; the later Op. 2 was engraved at Vienna in 1781 and dedicated to Josephine von Auernhammer, a talented pupil of Mozart. See Alfred Einstein, "Opus I," *Essays in Music*, by Einstein (New York: Norton, 1962), 47–49.

30. *The New Grove Dictionary of Music and Musicians*, s.v. "Mozart" by Stanley Sadie, 12: 697; Reeser, Preface, *NMA*, Serie VIII/23/1, x–xiii.

31. Wolfgang Plath, "Beiträge zur Mozart-Autographie II," *MJb 1976–77*, 169–71; Alan Tyson, "The Mozart Fragments in the Mozarteum, Salzburg: A Preliminary Study of Their Chronology and Significance," *The Journal of the American Musicological Society* 34 (Fall 1981): 476, reprinted in Alan Tyson, *Mozart, Studies of the Autograph Scores* (Cambridge: Harvard University Press, 1987). According to recent research by Alan Tyson as

well as by Wolfgang Plath and Wolfgang Rehm, in their edition of these sonatas for the *NMA*, the three sonatas may have been written as late as 1783 and perhaps in Salzburg, during Mozart's three-month visit. See Tyson, *Mozart, Studies*, 228–32; Wolfgang Plath and Wolfgang Rehm, Preface, *NMA*, Serie IX, *Klaviermusik*, Werkgruppe 25: *Klaviersonaten*, Band 2 (Kassel: Bärenreiter, 1986), viii–xii.

32. Türk, 377.

33. *The New Grove Dictionary of Music and Musicians*, s.v. "Mozart" by Santley Sadie, 12: 701. See Plath and Rehm, Preface, *NMA*, Serie IX/25/2, xii.

34. *The New Grove Dictionary of Music and Musicians*, s.v. "Antoine Laurent Baudron" by Paulette Letailleur, 2: 299; s.v. "Nicholas Dezède," by Leland Fox, 5: 412–13.

35. Wolfgang Plath, Preface, *NMA*, Serie IX, *Klaviermusik*, Werkgruppe 27: *Klavierstücke*, Band 2: *Einzelstücke für Klavier* (Kassel: Bärenreiter, 1982), xii–xv.

36. In a letter dated Salzburg, 29 Sept. 1777, in Anderson, 283.

37. In a letter dated Munich, 11 Oct. 1777, in Anderson, 308.

38. In a letter dated Paris, 20 July 1778, in Anderson, 573–74.

39. Plath, Preface, *NMA*, Serie IX/27/2, xiv.

40. Plath, Preface, *NMA*, Serie IX/27/2, xiv.

41. Hermann Abert, *W. A. Mozart: neu bearbeitete und erweiterte Ausgabe von Otto Jahns 'Mozart'* (Leipzig: Breitkopf und Härtel, 1955), 2: 126–27.

42. Einstein, *Mozart*, 270.

43. Einstein, *Mozart*, 270.

44. Einstein, *Mozart*, 271.

45. Composed for the Duc de Guines and his daughter, who played the flute and harp, respectively.

46. Robert D. Levin (*Who Wrote the Mozart Four-Wind Concertante?* [Stuyvesant, NY: Pendragon Press, 1988]) asserts in an exhaustive study of this piece that the *Sinfonia concertante* (for oboe, clarinet, horn, and bassoon) is based on a transcription (and to some degree an alteration) of the solo parts of Mozart's *Symphonie concertante* (known through the composer's correspondence but assumed lost) for flute, oboe, horn, and bassoon. The transcription and preparation of a new orchestral accompaniment probably dates from the period 1820–30 and may have been undertaken by the Parisian composer Alexandre-Pierre-François Boely (1785–1858). See also Martin Stähelin, "Zur Echtheitsproblematik der mozartschen Bläserkonzerte," *MJb 1971–72*, 56–62; Kurt Birsak, "Zur Konzertanten Sinfonie KV 297b/Anh. C. 14.01," *MJb 1971–72*, 63–67; Daniel N. Leeson and Robert D. Levin, "On the Authenticity of K. Anh. C. 14.01 (297b), a Symphonia Concertate for Four Winds and Orchestra," *MJb 1976–77*, 70–96.

47. See Christoph-Hellmut Mahling, Preface, *NMA*, Serie V, *Konzerte*, Werkgruppe 14: *Konzerte für ein oder mehrere Streich-, Blas- und Zupfinstrumente und Orchester*, Band 2: *Concertone, Sinfonia Concertante* (Kassel: Bärenreiter, 1975).

48. Research by Alan Tyson indicates that the cadenzas for the first and third movements of K. 365 (316a) are on a paper type that Mozart used for works dating conclusively from 1776 and 1777 and, therefore, suggests that the Concerto in E-flat Major K. 365 (316a) has an earlier origin. See Tyson, *Mozart, Studies*, 172, 345.

49. Christoph Wolff, Preface, *NMA*, Serie V, *Konzerte*, Werkgruppe 15: *Konzerte für ein oder mehrere Klaviere und Orchester mit Kadenzen*, Band 2 (Kassel: Bärenreiter, 1976), viii–ix.

50. Wolff, Preface, *NMA,* Serie V/15/2, viii–ix.

51. Wolff, Preface, *NMA,* Serie V/15/2, xiii.

52. Wolff, Preface, *NMA,* Serie V/15/2, viii–ix.

53. Eva Badura-Skoda and Paul Badura-Skoda, *Interpreting Mozart,* 197–208.

54. Charles Rosen, *The Classical Style: Haydn, Mozart, Beethoven* (New York: Viking, 1971), 192. See also Linda Faye Ferguson, "*Col Basso* and *Generalbass* in Mozart's Keyboard Concertos: Notation, Performance Theory, and Practice" (Ph.D. diss., Princeton University, 1983), esp. 1–99. Ferguson has examined in detail the variety and subtlety of performance possibilities suggested by Mozart's indications in the scores for all his concertos. See also Linda Faye Ferguson, "Mozart's Keyboard Concertos: Tutti Notations and Performance Models," *MJb 1984–85,* 32–39. And for a summary of current discussion of continuo practice in the concertos, see Robert D. Levin, "The Classical Era: Instrumental Ornamentation, Improvisation and Cadenzas," in *Performance Practice, Music After 1600,* ed. Howard Mayer Brown and Stanley Sadie (New York: Norton, 1989), 287–89.

4. THE VIENNA YEARS

1. In a letter dated Vienna, 11 Mar. 1781, in Anderson, 713–14.

2. In a letter dated Vienna, 9 May 1781, in Anderson, 727–29.

3. Cf. Finscher, "Bach," 9.

4. Cf. Finscher, "Bach," 9.

5. In a letter dated Vienna, 24 Mar. 1781, in Anderson, 716–19.

6. See Alfred Mann, "Zur Kontrapunktlehre Haydns und Mozarts," *MJb 1978–79,* 195–99. See also Alfred Mann, *Theory and Practice* (New York: Norton, 1987), 41–42, 48–50.

7. For Mozart's dedication to Haydn, see Deutsch, 250. The significance of Haydn's Op. 33 has been widely discussed; see Jens Peter Larsen, *The New Grove Dictionary of Music and Musicians,* s.v. "Joseph Haydn," 8: 354.

8. Cf. Nissen, 642.

9. Deutsch, 250.

10. *The New Grove Dictionary of Music and Musicians,* s.v. "Gottfried van Swieten" by Edward Olleson, 18: 414–15.

11. In a letter dated Vienna, 10 Apr. 1782, in Anderson, 799–800.

12. Einstein, *Mozart,* 156.

13. Cf. Finscher, "Bach," 12. See Warren Kirkendale, "More Slow Introductions by Mozart to Fugues of J. S. Bach," *Journal of the American Musicological Society* 17 (Spring 1964): 43–65. It is interesting to note that the source of Mozart's arrangements is now in the United States: MS 538 of the Riemenschneider collection, Riemenschneider Bach Institute, Baldwin-Wallace College, Berea, Ohio.

14. Cf. Finscher, "Bach," 13.

15. In a letter dated Vienna, 2 Apr. 1782, in Anderson, 800–801.

16. Einstein, *Mozart,* 152.

17. Cf. Finscher, "Bach," 12; Kirkendale, 44–46, 56.

18. Plath, Preface, *NMA,* Serie IX/27/2, xv–xvi.

19. Plath, Preface, *NMA,* Serie IX/27/2, xvi.

20. Plath, Preface, *NMA,* Serie IX/27/2, xv.

21. Plath, Preface, *NMA*, Serie IX/27/2, xxiv–xxv; Tyson, "Mozart Fragments," 489–91, 507–9, subsequently reprinted in Tyson, *Mozart, Studies; The New Grove Dictionary of Music and Musicians*, s.v. "Wolfgang Amadeus Mozart, Worklist" by Stanley Sadie, 12:745; Cf. Finscher, "Bach," 13.

22. Tyson, "Mozart Fragments," 497–99.

23. Plath, Preface, *NMA*, Serie IX/27/2, xviii.

24. Finscher, "Bach," 14.

25. Both the autograph manuscript of the Fugue in C Minor K. 426 for two pianos and Beethoven's copy of the fugue, on loan from Robert Owen Lehman, are in the collections of the Pierpont Morgan Library, New York. Also in the Morgan Library for an exhibit during the spring of 1984 was a portion of the finale of Mozart's String Quartet in G Major K. 387 in a score copy made by Beethoven, again for the purpose of study. During the eighteenth century, instrumental music was issued only in parts, making it necessary for one to assemble and copy out the parts into a score. Beethoven's copy of the Mozart quartet is part of the Mary Flager Cary Music Collection. The above information was kindly furnished by J. Rigbie Turner, curator of music manuscripts, Pierpont Morgan Library.

26. See the discussion of the various *opera* 1 and 2, chap. 3, n.29.

27. Einstein, *Mozart*, 257.

28. Karl Friedrich Cramer (*Magazin der Musik* [Hamburg], Apr. 1783), quoted in Einstein, *Mozart*, 256.

29. See the letter dated Vienna, 11 Apr. 1781, in Anderson, 722–24.

30. In a letter dated Vienna, 8 Apr. 1781, in Anderson, 721–22.

31. *The New Grove Dictionary of Music and Musicians*, s.v. "Wolfgang Amadeus Mozart, Worklist" by Stanley Sadie, 12: 743; Eduard Reeser, Preface, *NMA*, Serie VIII, *Kammermusik*, Werkgruppe 23: *Sonaten und Variationen für Klavier und Violine*, Band 2 (Kassel: Bärenreiter, 1965), xi–xiv.

32. In a letter dated Vienna, 10 Apr. 1784, in Anderson, 875.

33. Einstein, *Mozart*, 258.

34. In a letter dated Vienna, 10 Apr. 1784, in Anderson, 873.

35. One should remember that Mozart's advocacy of mean-tone temperament for orchestral instruments (see my later discussion in this chapter, p. 101) was suitable to the irregular temperament common to keyboard instruments in the period. Cf. John Hind Chesnut, "Mozart's Teaching of Intonation," *Journal of the American Musicological Society* 30 (Summer 1977): 254–71. See also Zaslaw, *Mozart's Symphonies*, 470.

36. Nissen, 633–34. Cf. Einstein, *Mozart*, 263–64.

37. Daniel Heartz and Alfred Mann, Critical Report to *NMA*, Serie X, *Supplement*, Werkgruppe 30: Band 1: *Thomas Attwoods Theorie- und Kompositionsstudien bei Mozart* (Kassel: Bärenreiter, 1969), 108.

38. See Rosen, *Classical Style*, 351–54.

39. *The New Grove Dictionary of Music and Musicians*, s.v. "Joseph Haydn, Worklist" by Georg Feder, 8: 388–89.

40. See Marie Rolf, "Stylistic Influence in the Early Haydn Piano Trios," in *Haydn Studies,* ed. by Jens Peter Larsen, Howard Serwer, and James Webster (New York: Norton, 1981), 459–64. See also Jerald C. Graue, "Haydn and the London Pianoforte School," in *Haydn Studies,* ed. Jens Peter Larsen, Howard Serwer, and James Webster (New York: Norton, 1981), 422–31.

41. Einstein, *Mozart*, 260.

42. Plath and Rehm, Preface, *NMA*, Serie VIII/22/2, x–xv.

43. Einstein, *Mozart*, 287.

44. Understandably, the concertos have been and continue to be the source of especially detailed study and research. The monograph *W. A. Mozart et ses concertos pour piano* by Cuthbert M. Girdlestone, published in 1939 (translated by the author as *Mozart's Piano Concertos* [New York: Dover, 1964]), was the first work devoted exclusively to the genre. *A Companion to Mozart's Piano Concertos* (1948) by Arthur Hutchings is a volume similar in plan but more modest in scope. In the bicentenary year 1956 appeared two studies, both contained in *The Mozart Companion*, a distinguished collection of essays: "The Concertos: Their Musical Origins and Development" by H. C. Robbins Landon is a stylistic précis tied to Mozart biography; the other essay, "The Concertos: Their Sources" by Friedrich Blume, examines summarily the background of the concerto manuscripts. Mention might also be made of the perceptive examination by Charles Rosen in the chapter "The Concerto" in his book *The Classical Style* and the fine analytical contributions of Donald Francis Tovey in the *Essays in Musical Analysis*. Other recent studies have variously considered aspects of form, structure, and performance in the concertos. See also prefaces and corresponding critical reports for the eight volumes of the piano concertos in the *NMA*, Serie V, Werkgruppe 15, Band 1–8. See also Eva Badura-Skoda and Paul Badura-Skoda, *Interpreting Mozart*, 242–90; Denis Forman, *Mozart's Concerto Form: The First Movements of the Piano Concertos* (New York: Praeger, 1971); Jane R. Stevens, "Theme, Harmony, and Texture in Classic-Romantic Descriptions of Concerto First-Movement Form, *Journal of the American Musicological Society* 27 (Spring 1974): 25–60; Neal Zaslaw, jacket notes, John Eliot Gardiner, cond.; Malcolm Bilson, fortepiano; English Baroque Soloists. *Mozart: Concertos for Piano(s) and Orchestra (23); Rondo for Piano and Orchestra (2)*, Archiv Produktion CD: 427 317–2 (1989); 413 464–2 (1984); 413–463–2 (1984); 415 525–2 (1986); 427 846–2 (1987, 1988, 1989); 415 990–2 (1987); 410 905–2 (1984); 415 525–2 (1986).

45. In a letter dated Salzburg, 24 Apr. 1792, from Johann Andreas Schachter to Maria Anna von Berchtold zu Sonnenberg [née Maria Anna Mozart, Mozart's sister], in Deutsch, 451–54.

46. Einstein, *Mozart*, 287.

47. In a letter dated Vienna, 28 Dec. 1782, in Anderson, 833–34.

48. In a letter dated Vienna, 26 Apr. 1783, in Anderson, 846. Cf. Wilhelm A. Bauer, Otto Erich Deutsch, and Joseph H. Eibl, eds. *Mozart: Briefe und Aufzeichnungen* (Kassel: Bärenreiter, 1963), 3: 266.

49. See Christoph Wolff, Preface, *NMA*, Serie V, *Konzerte*, Werkgruppe 15: *Konzerte für ein oder mehrere Klaviere und Orchester mit Kadenzen*, Band 3 (Kassel: Bärenreiter, 1976), ix.

50. For a discussion of the possible stylistic and chronological connections between the concertos of 1782–83 and K. 449, see Tyson, "Mozart Fragments," 501–5. There is strong evidence to support the argument that the Rondo in A major K. 386, long considered to have been written by Mozart as a possible alternate finale to the Concerto in A major K. 414 (385p), was actually conceived as an independent concert rondo. See Tyson, *Mozart, Studies*, 262–89.

51. Rosen, *Classical Style*, 219. For a discussion of the evolution and chronology of K. 449, see Tyson, *Mozart, Studies*, 153–57.

52. Einstein, *Mozart*, 302.

53. In a letter dated Vienna, 26 May 1784, in Anderson, 877–79.

54. In a letter dated Vienna, 9 June 1784, in Anderson, 879–80. See also Marius Flothuis, Preface, *NMA*, Serie V, *Konzerte*, Werkgruppe 15: *Konzerte für ein oder mehrere Klaviere und Orchester mit Kadenzen*, Band 4 (Kassel: Bärenreiter, 1975), x–xi.

55. In a letter dated Vienna, 26 May 1784, in Anderson, 877–79.

56. See the first movement, measures 88–91, *NMA*, Serie V/15/6, 10–11. See also Hans Engel and Horst Heussner, Preface, *NMA*, Serie V, *Konzerte*, Werkgruppe 15: *Konzerte für ein oder mehrere Klaviere und Orchester mit Kadenzen*, Band 6 (Kassel: Bärenreiter, 1961), xix–xv.

57. In a letter dated Vienna, 12 Mar. 1785, in Anderson, 888–89.

58. Einstein, *Mozart*, 309.

59. Einstein, *Mozart*, 310.

60. H. C. Robbins Landon, *Mozart, The Golden Years, 1781–1791* (New York: Schirmer Books, 1989), 32–35.

61. Alan Tyson, "Redating Mozart: Some Stylistic and Biographical Implications," Papers read at the forty-ninth annual meeting of the American Musicological Society, Louisville, Ky., 27–30 Oct. 1983.

62. Tyson, "Redating Mozart."

63. See Tyson, "Mozart Fragments," 487–89, 495–505.

64. See Eva Badura-Skoda and Paul Badura-Skoda, *Interpreting Mozart*, 266–79.

65. For a discussion concerning embellishment and elaboration in the piano works, see Levin, "Classical Era," 269–87; Frederick Neumann, *Ornamentation and Improvisation in Mozart* (Princeton: Princeton University Press, 1986), 240–56; Eva Badura-Skoda and Paul Badura-Skoda, *Interpreting Mozart*, 177–96.

66. *The Grove Dictionary of Music and Musicians*, s.v. "Wolfgang Amadeus Mozart, Worklist" by Stanley Sadie, 12: 744. See Alan Tyson, "The Date of Mozart's Piano Sonata in B-flat major, KV 333/315c: The 'Linz' Sonata?," in *Musik, Edition, Interpretation: Gedenkschrift Günter Henle*, ed. Martin Bente (Munich: G. Henle Verlag, 1980), 447–54; Plath, "Beiträge zur Mozart-Autographie II," 171.

67. *The Grove Dictionary of Music and Musicians*, s.v. "Wolfgang Amadeus Mozart" by Stanley Sadie, 12: 714.

68. *The Grove Dictionary of Music and Musicians*, s.v. "Wolfgang Amadeus Mozart" by Stanley Sadie, 12: 706.

69. Plath, Preface, *NMA*, Serie IX/27/2, xxv–xxvi.

70. In a letter dated Vienna, 12 Jan. 1782, in Anderson, 791–92. Wyzewa and Saint-Foix, and Einstein have all noted Mozart's appraisal of Clementi; see, however, the discussion of Clementi's influence with respect to the solo keyboard variations K. 500, p. 104.

71. *The New Grove Dictionary of Music and Musicians*, s.v. "Fantasia, 18th century" by Eugene Helm, 6: 389. See also Georges de Saint-Foix, "Le problème de la fantasie en ut mineur de Mozart [Koechel 396]," *Revue belge de musicologie* 3 (1949): 219–21; Jesse Parker, "The Clavier Fantasy from Mozart to Liszt" (Ph.D. diss., Stanford University, 1974), 14–15, 19–23.

72. Plath, Preface, *NMA*, Serie IX/27/2, xvi.

73. Alec Hyatt King. *Mozart in Retrospect: Studies in Criticism and Bibliography* (London: Oxford University Press, 1955), 256.

74. *The New Grove Dictionary of Music and Musicians,* s.v. "Temperaments" by Mark Lindley, 18: 667.

75. Einstein, *Mozart,* 248.

76. See Plath, Preface, *NMA,* Serie IX/27/2, xxix. See also Eric Schenk, "Ein unbekanntes Klavier-Übungsstück Mozarts," in *Collectanea Mozartiana,* ed. Mozart Gemeinde Wien (Tutzing: Hans Schneider, 1988), 139–48.

77. Jean-Pierre Duport (1741–1818), French cellist and composer in the employ of the Prussian monarchs beginning with Frederick the Great. Mozart became acquainted with the minuet from the Sonata for Cello, Op. 4, no. 6, during his visit to Potsdam in 1789.

78. In a letter dated Vienna, 29 Mar. 1783, in Anderson, 843–44.

79. Abert, 2: 310.

80. Jerald C. Graue, "Muzio Clementi and the Development of Pianoforte Music in Industrial England" (Ph.D. diss., University of Illinois, 1971), 109. See chap. 4, n. 70.

81. Graue, "Muzio Clementi," 99.

82. Abert, 2: 598.

5. THE LAST PHASE

1. Einstein, *Mozart,* 313.

2. Rosen, *Classical Style,* 258.

3. Rosen, *Classical Style,* 258.

4. See Christoph Wolff, "Zur Chronologie der Klavierkonzert-Kadenzen Mozarts," *MJb 1978–79,* 235–46.

5. Wolff, "Zur Chronologie," 245–46.

6. See Wolfgang Rehm, Preface, *NMA,* Serie V, *Konzerte,* Werkgruppe 15: *Konzerte für ein oder mehrere Klaviere und Orchester mit Kadenzen,* Band 8 (Kassel: Bärenreiter, 1960), xxiii–xxiv.

7. Rosen, *Classical Style,* 260.

8. Plath, Preface, *NMA,* Serie IX/27/2, xvi–xvii.

9. Plath, "Zur Echtheitsfrage bei Mozart," *MJb 1971–72,* 30–31.

10. Einstein, *Mozart,* 250.

11. Plath, Preface, *NMA,* Serie IX/27/2, p. xvii.

12. Friedrich Rochlitz, "Anekdoten aus Mozarts Leben," in David and Mendel, 359–60.

13. Plath, Preface, *NMA,* Serie IX/27/2, xviii.

14. See Mann, "Zur Kontrapunktlehre," 195–99. See also Erich Hertzmann, Cecil B. Oldman, Daniel Heartz, and Alfred Mann, Preface, *NMA,* Serie X, *Supplement,* Werkgruppe 30: Band 1: *Thomas Attwoods Theorie- und Kompositionsstudien bei Mozart* (Kassel: Bärenreiter, 1965); Hellmut Federhofer and Alfred Mann, Preface, *NMA,* Serie X, *Supplement,* Werkgruppe 30: Band 2: *Barbara Ployers und Franz Jacob Freystädtlers Theorie- und Kompositionsstudien bei Mozart* (Leipzig: VEB Deutscher Verlag für Musik, 1989).

15. Plath, Preface, *NMA,* Serie IX/27/2, xviii.

16. Cf. Finscher, "Bach," 15.

17. Plath, Preface, *NMA,* Serie IX/27/2, xviii.

18. Wolff, Preface, *NMA,* Serie V/15/2, viii.

19. See H. C. Robbins Landon, *The Symphonies of Joseph Haydn* (London: Universal Editions and Rockliff Publishing, 1955), 594–604.

20. See Rehm, Preface, *NMA,* Serie V/15/8, xxiv–xxvi.

21. Rehm, Preface, *NMA,* Serie V/15/8, xxv–xxvi.

22. Einstein, *Mozart,* 314.

Bibliography

✳

The abbreviation *MJb* refers to the *Mozart Jahrbuch* (Salzburg, 1950–), a yearly publication issued by the Internationale Stiftung Mozarteum, and the abbreviation *NMA* refers to *Wolfgang Amadeus Mozart: Neue Ausgabe sämtlicher Werke* (Kassel: Bärenreiter, 1956–91), the critical edition of Mozart's works.

Abert, Hermann. *W. A. Mozart: neu bearbeitete und erweiterte Ausgabe von Otto Jahns 'Mozart'*. 2d ed. 2 vols. Leipzig: Breitkopf und Härtel, 1955.

Agricola, Johann Friedrich. "Bach on Silbermann's Pianofortes." In *The Bach Reader*, edited by Hans T. David and Arthur Mendel. New York: Norton, 1966.

Anderson, Emily. *The Letters of Mozart and His Family*. 3d edition corrected by Stanley Sadie and Fiona Smart, after the 2d edition prepared by A. Hyatt King and Monica Carolan. New York: Norton, 1985.

Angermüller, Rudolph. *Mozart und seine Welt*. Kassel: Bärenreiter, 1979.

Bach, Carl Philipp Emanuel. *Essay on the True Art of Playing Keyboard Instruments*. Translated and edited by William J. Mitchell. New York: Norton, 1949.

Badura-Skoda, Eva. "Clementi's 'Musical Characteristics' opus 19." In *Studies in Eighteenth-Century Music, A Tribute to Karl Geiringer on his Seventieth Birthday*, edited by H. C. Robbins Landon and Roger E. Chapman, 53–67. London: George Allen and Unwin, 1970.

———. "Haydn, Mozart and Their Contemporaries." Translated by Margaret Bent. In *Keyboard Music*, edited by Denis Matthews, 108–65. Newton Abbot, England: David and Charles, 1972.

———. "Komponierte J. S. Bach 'Hammerklavier-Konzerte'?" *Bach Jahrbuch 1990–91*, 159–71.

———. "Prolegomena to a History of the Viennese Fortepiano." *Israel Studies in Musicology* 2 (1980): 77–99.

———. "Zur Frühgeschichte des Hammerklaviers." *Florilegium Musicologium: Festschrift Hellmut Federhofer*. Tutzing: Hans Schneider Verlag, 1988.

Badura-Skoda, Eva, and Paul Badura-Skoda. *Interpreting Mozart on the Keyboard*. Translated by Leo Black. New York: St. Martin's, 1962.

———. Preface. *NMA*, Serie V, *Konzerte*, Werkgruppe 15: *Konzerte für ein oder mehrere Klaviere und Orchester mit Kadenzen*, Band 5. Kassel: Bärenreiter, 1965.

Badura-Skoda, Paul. "Ein authentischer Eingang zum Klavierkonzert in B-Dur, KV 595?" *MJb 1971–72*, 76–80.

———. *Kadenzen, Eingänge und Auszierungen zu Klavierkonzerten von Wolfgang Amadeus Mozart.* Kassel: Bärenreiter, 1967.

Bauer, Wilhelm A., Otto Erich Deutsch, and Joseph H. Eibl, eds. *Mozart: Briefe und Aufzeichnungen.* 7 vols. Kassel: Bärenreiter, 1962–75.

Beck, Hermann. Preface. *NMA, Serie V, Konzerte,* Werkgruppe 15: *Konzerte für ein oder mehrere Klaviere und Orchester mit Kadenzen,* Band 7. Kassel: Bärenreiter, 1959.

Bilson, Malcolm. "The Classical Era: Keyboards." In *Performance Practice, Music After 1600,* edited by Howard Mayer Brown and Stanley Sadie, 223–38. New York: Norton, 1989.

———. "The Mozart Concertos Rediscovered." *MJb 1986,* 58–61.

Birsak, Kurt. "Zur Konzertanten Sinfonie KV 297b/Anh. C. 14.01." *MJb 1971–72,* 63–67.

Blom, Eric. *The Romance of the Piano.* London: G. T. Foulis, 1928; New York: Da Capo Press, 1969.

Blume, Friedrich. "The Concertos: Their Sources." In *The Mozart Companion,* edited by H. C. Robbins Landon and Donald Mitchell, 200–233. New York: Norton, 1969.

Blume, Friedrich, and Hans Redlich, eds. *Wolfgang Amadeus Mozart: Concertos for Piano and Orchestra.* 3 vols. London: Ernst Eulenberg, n.d.

Bockholdt, Rudolf. "Zur neuen Funktion von Klavier und Orchester in den Mittelsätzen von Mozarts Klavierkonzerten seit 1784." *MJb 1986,* 61–71.

Braunbehrens, Volkmar. *Mozart in Wien.* Munich: R. Piper GmbH, 1986.

Broder, Nathan. "Mozart and the 'Clavier,' " In *The Creative World of Mozart,* edited by Paul Henry Lang, 76–85. New York: Norton, 1964.

Brown, A. Peter. *Joseph Haydn's Keyboard Music, Sources and Style.* Bloomington: Indiana University Press, 1986.

Burde, Wolfgang. *Studien zu Mozarts Klaviersonaten: Formungsprinzipien und Formtypen.* Giebing über Prien am Chiemsee: Musikverlag Katzbichler, 1969.

Chesnut, John Hind. "Mozart's Teaching of Intonation." *Journal of the American Musicological Society* 30 (Summer 1977): 254–71.

David, Hans T., and Arthur Mendel, eds. *The Bach Reader.* New York: Norton, 1966.

Day, James, and Peter le Huray, eds. *Music and Aesthetics in the Eighteenth and Early-Nineteenth Centuries.* Cambridge: Cambridge University Press, 1981.

Dennerlein, Hanns. "Mozarts europäische Orgelerfahrung." *MJb 1978–79,* 269–75.

———. *Der unbekannte Mozart: Die Welt seiner Klavierwerke.* Leipzig: Breitkopf und Härtel, 1955.

Deutsch, Otto Erich. *Mozart, A Documentary Biography.* Translated by Eric Blom, Peter Branscombe, and Jeremy Noble. London: Adam and Charles Black, 1965.

Einstein, Alfred. *Mozart, His Character, His Work.* Translated by Arthur Mendel and Nathan Broder. London: Oxford University Press, 1945.

———. "Opus I." *Essays in Music.* By Einstein. 49–63. New York: Norton, 1962. 39–63.

Eisen, Cliff. "Contributions to a New Mozart Documentary Biography." *Journal of the American Musicological Society* 39 (Fall 1986): 615–32.

———. "Leopold Mozart Discoveries." *Mitteilungen der Internationalen Stiftung Mozarteum* 35 (July 1987): 1–10.

———. "Mozart Apocrypha." *The Musical Times* 127 (Dec. 1986): 683–85.

———. "New Light on Mozart's 'Linz' Symphony, K. 425." *Journal of the Royal Musical Association* 113 (1988): 81–96.

———. "Some Lost Mozart Editions of the 1780s." *Mitteilungen der Internationalen Stiftung Mozarteum* 32 (1984): 64–70.

Engel, Hans, and Horst Heussner. Preface. *NMA*, Serie V, *Konzerte*, Werkgruppe 15: *Konzerte für ein oder mehrere Klaviere und Orchester mit Kadenzen*, Band 6. Kassel: Bärenreiter, 1961.

Federhofer, Hellmut. "Mozart als Schüler und Lehrer." *MJb 1970–71*, 89–106.

———. Preface. *NMA*, Serie VIII, *Kammermusik*, Werkgruppe 22: *Quintette, Quartette und Trios mit Klavier und mit Glassharmonika*, Abteilung 1: *Quartette und Quintette mit Klavier und mit Glassharmonika*. Kassel: Bärenreiter, 1957.

Federhofer, Hellmut, and Alfred Mann. Preface. *NMA*, Serie X, *Supplement*, Werkgruppe 30: Band 2: *Barbara Ployers und Franz Jacob Freystädtlers Theorie- und Kompositionsstudien bei Mozart*. Kassel: Bärenreiter and Leipzig: VEB Deutscher Verlag für Musik, 1989.

Ferguson, Linda Faye. "*Col Basso* und *Generalbass* in Mozart's Keyboard Concertos: Notation, Performance Theory, and Practice." Ph.D. diss., Princeton University, 1983.

———. "Mozart's Keyboard Concertos: Tutti Notations and Performance Models." *MJb 1984–85*, 32–39.

Finscher, Ludwig. "Bach und die Wiener Klassik." *Bach-Tage, Vorträge 1975*. Berlin: published with the program book Bach-Tage, 1977.

———. "Mozarts erstes Streichquartett: Lodi, 15. März 1770." *Analecta Musicologica: Colloquium "Mozart und Italien" (Rom 1974)*, edited by Friedrich Lippmann, 246–70. Köln: Arno Volk Verlag Hans Gerig KG, 1978.

Fischer, Wilhelm. "Mozarts Weg von den begleiten Klaviersonaten zur Kammermusik mit Klavier." *MJb 1956*, 16–34.

Flothuis, Marius. "Bühne und Konzert." *MJb 1986*, 45–58.

———. Preface. *NMA*, Serie V, *Konzerte*, Werkgruppe 15: *Konzerte für ein oder mehrere Klaviere und Orchester mit Kadenzen*, Band 1. Kassel: Bärenreiter, 1972.

———. Preface. *NMA*, Serie V, *Konzerte*, Werkgruppe 15: *Konzerte für ein order mehrere Klaviere und Orchester mit Kadenzen*, Band 4. Kassel: Bärenreiter, 1975.

Flotzinger, Rudolf. "Die Klaviervariationen W. A. Mozarts in der Tradition des 18. Jahrhunderts." *Mitteilungen der Internationalen Stiftung Mozarteum* (Aug. 1975): 13–27.

Forman, Denis. *Mozart's Concerto Form: The First Movements of the Piano Concertos*. New York: Praeger, 1971.

Forster, Robert. "Zur Funktion von Anfangsritornell und Reprise in den Kopfsätzen einiger Klavierkonzerte Mozarts." *MJb 1986*, 74–89.

Frederick, Michael E. "English vs. Viennese Fortepianos." *Haydn's Piano Sonatas*. Westfield, Mass.: Westfield Center for Early Keyboard Studies, 1990.

Gärtner, Heinz. *Johann Christian Bach, Mozarts Freund und Lehrmeister*. Munich: Nymphenberger, F. A. Herbig Verlagsbuchhandlung GmbH, 1989.

Gerstenberg, Walter. Preface. *NMA*, Serie X, *Supplement*, Werkgruppe 28: *Bearbeitungen, Ergänzungen und Übertragungen fremder Werke*, Abteilung 2: *Bearbeitungen von Werken verschiedener Komponisten, Klavierkonzerte und Kadenzen*. Kassel: Bärenreiter, 1964.

Girdlestone, Cuthbert M. *Mozart's Piano Concertos*. New York: Dover, 1964.

Graue, Jerald C. "Haydn and the London Pianoforte School." In *Haydn Studies,* edited by Jens Peter Larsen, Howard Serwer, and James Webster, 422–31. New York: Norton, 1981.

———. "Muzio Clementi and the Development of Pianoforte Music in Industrial England." Ph.D. diss., University of Illinois, 1971.

Haberkamp, Gertraut. *Die Erstdrucke der Werke von Wolfgang Amadeus Mozart.* Tutzing: Hans Schneider, 1986.

Hamann, Heinz Wolfgang. "Mozarts Schülerkreis." *MJb 1962–63,* 115–39.

Hausner, Henry H. "Franz Anton Hoffmeister (1754–1812), Komponist und Verleger." *Mitteilungen der Internationalen Stiftung Mozarteum* 38 (July 1990): 155–62.

Heartz, Daniel, and Alfred Mann. Critical Report. *NMA,* Serie X, *Supplement,* Werkgruppe 30: Band 1: *Thomas Attwoods Theorie- und Kompositionsstudien bei Mozart.* Kassel: Bärenreiter, 1969.

Hertzmann, Erich, Cecil B. Oldman, Daniel Heartz and Alfred Mann. Preface. *NMA,* Serie X, *Supplement,* Werkgruppe 30: Band 1: *Thomas Attwoods Theorie- und Kompositionsstudien bei Mozart.* Kassel: Bärenreiter, 1965.

Hildesheimer, Wolfgang. *Mozart.* Frankfurt: Suhrkamp Verlag, 1977.

Hogwood, Christopher. Introduction. *J. C. Bach: Twelve Keyboard Sonatas (Opera V).* [London:] Oxford University Press, 1973.

Hutchings, Arthur. *A Companion to Mozart's Piano Concertos.* London: Oxford University Press, 1948.

———. "The Keyboard Music." In *The Mozart Companion,* edited by H. C. Robbins Landon and Donald Mitchell, 32–65. New York: Norton, 1969.

Jackson, Timothy. "Mozart's 'Little Gigue' in G major K. 574: A Study in Rhythmic Shift—A Reminiscence of the Competition with Häßler." *Mitteilungen der Internationalen Stiftung Mozarteum* 37 (July 1989): 70–80.

Kecskeméti, István. "Opernelemente in den Klavierkonzerten Mozarts." *MJb 1968–70,* 111–18.

Kelly, Michael. *Reminiscences of Michael Kelly.* Reprint volume edited with an introduction by Roger Fiske. London, 1826; London: Oxford University Press, 1975.

Kenyon, Nicholas, ed. *Authenticity and Early Music.* Oxford: Oxford University Press, 1988.

Kerman, Joseph, ed. *Mozart: Piano Concerto in C major K. 503.* New York: Norton, 1970.

King, Alec Hyatt. *Mozart in Retrospect: Studies in Criticism and Bibliography.* London: Oxford University Press, 1955.

———. *A Mozart Legacy, Aspects of the British Library Collections.* Seattle: University of Washington Press, 1984.

———. "Mozart Literature." In *The Mozart Compendium, A Guide to Mozart's Life and Music,* edited by H. C. Robbins Landon, 404–20. New York: Schirmer Books, 1990.

Kirby, F. E. *A Short History of Keyboard Music.* New York: Free Press, 1966.

Kirkendale, Warren. "More Slow Introductions by Mozart to Fugues of J. S. Bach." *Journal of the American Musicological Society* 17 (Spring 1964): 43–65.

Köchel, Ludwig Ritter von. *Chronologisch-thematisches Verzeichnis sämtlicher Tonwerke Wolfgang Amadé Mozarts.* Leipzig, 1862; 2d ed. prepared by P. Graf von Waldersee, 1905; 3d ed. prepared by A. Einstein, 1937; reprints of 3d ed. with supplement,

1947; 4th ed., 1958; 5th ed., 1963; 6th ed. prepared by F. Giegling, A. Weinmann, and G. Sievers, 1964; 7th ed., 1965.

Landon, H. C. Robbins. "The Concertos: Their Musical Origins and Development." In *The Mozart Companion*, edited by H. C. Robbins Landon and Donald Mitchell, 234–82. New York: Norton, 1969.

———. *Haydn: Chronicle and Works.* 5 vols. Bloomington: Indiana University Press, 1976–80.

———. *The Mozart Compendium, A Guide to Mozart's Life and Music.* New York: Schirmer Books, 1990.

———. *Mozart, The Golden Years 1781–1791.* New York: Schirmer Books, 1989.

———. *1791, Mozart's Last Year.* New York: Schirmer Books, 1988.

———. *The Symphonies of Joseph Haydn.* London: Universal Edition and Rockliff Publishing, 1955.

Lang, Paul Henry. *Music in Western Civilization.* New York: Norton, 1941.

Larsen, Jens Peter. "Some Observations on the Development and Characteristics of Vienna Classical Instrumental Music." *Studia Musicologica* 9 (1967): 115–39.

———. "The Symphonies." In *The Mozart Companion*, edited by H. C. Robbins Landon and Donald Mitchell, 156–99. New York: Norton, 1969.

La Rue, Jan. Introduction. *Mozart: Piano Concerto No. 21 in C Major, K. 467, The Autograph Score.* New York: Pierpont Morgan Library and Dover, 1985.

Leeson, Daniel N., and Robert D. Levin. "On the Authenticity of K. Anh. C. 14.01 (297b), A Symphonia Concertante for Four Winds and Orchestra." *MJb 1976–77,* 70–96.

Levarie, Siegmund. "Mozarts höchster Klavierton." *Mitteilungen der Internationalen Stiftung Mozarteum* 37 (July 1989): 45–51.

Levin, Robert D. "The Classical Era: Instrumental Ornamentation, Improvisation and Cadenzas." In *Performance Practice, Music After 1600*, edited by Howard Mayer Brown and Stanley Sadie, 267–91. New York: Norton, 1989.

———. "Improvisation and Embellishment in Mozart's Piano Concertos." *Musical Newsletter* 5 (Spring 1975): 3–14.

———. *Who Wrote the Mozart Four-Wind Concertante?* Stuyvesant, N.Y.: Pendragon Press, 1988.

Lindley, Mark. "The Baroque Era: Tuning and Intonation. In *Performance Practice, Music After 1600*, edited by Howard Mayer Brown and Stanley Sadie, 169–85. New York: Norton, 1989.

Mahling, Christoph-Hellmut. Preface. *NMA,* Serie V, *Konzerte,* Werkgruppe 14: *Konzerte für ein oder mehrere Streich-, Blas- und Zupfinstrumente und Orchester,* Band 2: *Concertone, Sinfonia Concertante.* Kassel: Bärenreiter, 1975.

Mann, Alfred. "Leopold Mozart als Lehrer seines Sohnes." *MJb 1989–90,* 31–36.

———. *Theory and Practice.* New York: Norton, 1987.

———. "Zum Salzburger Studienbuch." *MJb 1984–85,* 71–75.

———. "Zur Kontrapunktlehre Haydns und Mozarts." *MJb 1978–79,* 195–99.

Marguerre, K. "Die beiden Sonaten-Reihen für Klavier und Geige." *MJb 1968–70,* 327–31.

———. "Mozarts Klaviertrios." *MJb 1960–61,* 182–94.

Mies, Paul. "Die Artikulationszeichen Strich und Punkt bei Wolfgang Amadeus Mozart." *Die Musikforschung* 11 (1958): 428–55.

Milligan, Thomas B. *The Concerto and London's Musical Culture in the Late Eighteenth Cen-*

tury. Ph.D. diss., University of Rochester, 1979; Ann Arbor: UMI Research Press, 1983.

Mishkin, Henry G. "Incomplete Notation in Mozart's Piano Concertos." *Musical Quarterly* 61 (July 1975): 345–59.

Mitchell, William J. Introduction. *Essay on the True Art of Playing Keyboard Instruments*. By Carl Philipp Emanuel Bach. Translated and edited by William J. Mitchell. New York: Norton, 1949.

Mozart, Leopold. *A Treatise on the Fundamental Principles of Violin Playing*. Translated by Editha Knocker. 2d ed. London: Oxford University Press, 1963.

Neumann, Frederick. *Ornamentation and Improvisation in Mozart*. Princeton: Princeton University Press, 1986.

The New Grove Dictionary of Musical Instruments. Edited by Stanley Sadie. 3 vols. New York: Grove Dictionaries of Music, 1984.

The New Grove Dictionary of Music and Musicians. Edited by Stanley Sadie. 20 vols. London: MacMillan, 1980.

Newman, William S. *Beethoven on Beethoven: Playing His Piano His Way*. New York: Norton, 1988.

———. "Beethoven's Piano Versus His Piano Ideals." *Journal of the American Musicological Society* 29 (Fall 1970): 484–504.

———. *The Sonata in the Classic Era*. Chapel Hill: University of North Carolina Press, 1963.

Nissen, Georg Nikolaus von. *Biographie W. A. Mozarts*. Leipzig, 1828; facsimile ed., Hildesheim: Georg Olms Verlagsbuchhandlung, 1964.

Parker, Jesse. "The Clavier Fantasy from Mozart to Liszt." Ph.D. diss., Stanford University, 1974.

Parrish, Carl. "Criticisms of the Piano When It Was New." *Musical Quarterly* 30 (1944): 428–40.

———. "Haydn and the Piano," *Journal of the American Musicological Society* 1 (1948): 27–34.

Perry-Camp, Jane. "Divers Marks in Mozart's Autograph Manuscripts: Census and Significance." *MJb 1984–85*, 80–108.

Pestelli, Giorgio. *The Age of Mozart and Beethoven*. Translated by Eric Cross. Cambridge: Cambridge University Press, 1984.

Plantinga, Leon. *Clementi: His Life and Music*. London: Oxford University Press, 1977.

Plath, Wolfgang. "Beiträge zur Mozart-Autographie I: Die Handschrift Leopold Mozarts." *MJb 1960–61*, 82–117.

———. "Beiträge zur Mozart-Autographie II: Schriftchronologie 1770–1780." *MJb 1976–77*, 131–73.

———. "Leopold Mozarts Notenbuch für Wolfgang (1762)—eine Fälschung?" *MJb 1971–72*, 337–41.

———. Preface. *NMA*, Serie IX, *Klaviermusik*, Werkgruppe 27: *Klavierstücke*, Band 1: *Die Notenbücher*. Kassel: Bärenreiter, 1982.

———. Preface. *NMA*, Serie IX, *Klaviermusik*, Werkgruppe 27: *Klavierstücke*, Band 2: *Einzelstücke für Klavier*. Kassel: Bärenreiter, 1982.

———. "Zur Datierung der Klaviersonaten KV 279–284," *Acta Mozartiana* 21 (Aug. 1974): 26–30.

————. "Zur Echtheitsfrage bei Mozart." *MJb 1971–72*, 19–36.

Plath, Wolfgang, and Wolfgang Rehm. Preface. *NMA*, Serie VIII, *Kammermusik*, Werkgruppe 22: Abteilung 2: *Klaviertrios*. Kassel: Bärenreiter, 1966.

————. Preface. *NMA*, Serie IX, *Klaviermusik*, Werkgruppe 25: *Klaviersonaten*, Band 1. Kassel: Bärenreiter, 1986.

————. Preface. *NMA*, Serie IX, *Klaviermusik*, Werkgruppe 25: *Klaviersonaten*, Band 2. Kassel: Bärenreiter, 1986.

Reeser, Eduard. Preface. *NMA*, Serie VIII, *Kammermusik*, Werkgruppe 23: *Sonaten und Variationen für Klavier und Violine*, Band 1. Kassel: Bärenreiter, 1964.

————. Preface. *NMA*, Serie VIII, *Kammermusik*, Werkgruppe 23: *Sonaten und Variationen für Klavier und Violine*, Band 2. Kassel: Bärenreiter, 1965.

————. Preface. *NMA*, Serie X, *Supplement*, Werkgruppe 28: *Bearbeitungen, Ergänzungen und Übertragungen fremder Werke*, Abteilung 2: *Bearbeitungen von Werken verschiedener Komponisten, Klavierkonzerte und Kadenzen*. Kassel: Bärenreiter, 1964.

Rehm, Wolfgang. Preface. *NMA*, Serie V, *Konzerte*, Werkgruppe 15: *Konzerte für ein oder mehrere Klaviere und Orchester mit Kadenzen*, Band 8. Kassel: Bärenreiter, 1960.

————. Preface. *NMA*, Serie IX, *Klaviermusik*, Werkgruppe 24: *Werke für zwei Klaviere und für Klavier zu vier Händen*, Abteilung 2: *Werke für Klavier zu vier Händen*. Kassel: Bärenreiter, 1955.

Riggs, Robert Daniel. "Articulation in Mozart's and Beethoven's Sonatas for Piano and Violin: Source-Critical and Analytic Studies." Ph.D. diss., Harvard University, 1987.

Rolf, Marie. "Stylistic Influence in the Early Haydn Piano Trios." In *Haydn Studies,* edited by Jens Peter Larsen, Howard Serwer, and James Webster, 459–64. New York: Norton, 1981.

Rosen, Charles. *The Classical Style: Haydn, Mozart, Beethoven.* New York: Viking, 1971.

————. *Sonata Forms.* New York: Norton, 1980.

Rosenberg, Richard. *Die Klaviersonaten Mozarts: Gestalt- und Stilanalyse.* Hofheim am Taunus: F. Hofmeister, 1972.

Rosenblum, Sandra P. *Performance Practices in Classic Piano Music.* Bloomington: Indiana University Press, 1988.

Rücke, Ulrich. "Mozarts Hammerflügel erbaute Anton Walter, Wien." *MJb 1955*, 246–62.

Sadie, Stanley. *The New Grove Mozart.* New York: Norton, 1982.

Saint-Foix, Georges de. "Le problème de la fantasie en ut mineur de Mozart [Koechel 396]." *Revue belge de musicologie* 3 (1949): 219–21.

Schenk, Erich. "Ein unbekanntes Klavier-Übungsstück Mozarts." *Collectanea Mozartiana*, edited by The Mozart Gemeinde Wien, 139–48. Tutzing: Hans Schneider, 1988.

Schmid, Ernst Fritz. Preface. *NMA*, Serie IX, *Klaviermusik*, Werkgruppe 24: *Werke für zwei Klaviere und für Klavier zu vier Händen:* Abteilung 1: *Werke für zwei Klaviere*. Kassel: Bärenreiter, 1955.

Schmid, Manfred Hermann. "Nannerl Mozart und ihr musikalischer Nachlaß: Zu den Klavierkonzerten im Archiv St. Peter in Salzburg." *MJb 1980–83*, 140–47.

Schulenberg, David. *The Instrumental Music of Carl Philipp Emanuel Bach.* Ph.D. diss., State University of New York, Stony Brook, 1982; Ann Arbor: UMI Research Press, 1984.

Schuler, Heinz. "Mozarts Akademien im Trattnersaal 1784. Ein Kommentar zum Mozart-

Brief: Wien, 20. März 1784." *Mitteilungen der Internationalen Stiftung Mozarteum* 38 (July 1990): 1–48.

Senn, Walter. "Abbé Maximilian Stadler: Mozarts Nachlaß und das 'Unterrichtsheft' KV 453b." *MJb 1980–83*, 287–98.

———. "Mozart, Schüler und Bekannte." *MJb 1976–77*, 281–88.

Simon, Edwin J. "Sonata into Concerto: A Study of Mozart's First Seven Concertos." *Acta Musicologica* 31 (1959): 170–85.

Stähelin, Martin. "Zur Echtheitsproblematik der mozartschen Bläserkonzerte." *MJb 1971–72*, 56–62.

Stevens, Jane R. "Theme, Harmony, and Texture in Classic-Romantic Descriptions of Concerto First-Movement Form." *Journal of the American Musicological Society* 27 (Spring 1974): 25–60.

Strohm, Reinhard. "Merkmale italienischer Versvertonung in Mozarts Klavierkonzerten." *Analecta Musicologica: Colloquium "Mozart und Italien" (Rom 1974)*, edited by Friedrich Lippmann, 219–36. Köln: Arno Volk Verlag Hans Gerig KG, 1978.

Sulzer, Johann Georg. "Allgemeine Theorie der schönen Künste," 2nd edn. 1792–94. In *Music and Aesthetics in the Eighteenth and Early-Nineteenth Centuries*, edited by James Day and Peter le Huray, 120–39. Cambridge: Cambridge University Press, 1981.

Temperley, Nicholas. "Mozart's Influence on English Music." *Music and Letters* 42 (1961): 307–18.

Terry, Charles Sanford. *John Christian Bach*. London: Oxford University Press, 1929.

Türk, Daniel Gottlob. *Klavierschule*. Leipzig & Halle, 1789; facsimile ed. Erwin R. Jacobi, Kassel: Bärenreiter, 1967; *School of Clavier Playing, or, Instructions in Playing the Clavier for Teachers and Students by Daniel Gottlob Türk*. Trans. with notes by Raymond H. Haggh. Lincoln: University of Nebraska Press, 1982.

Turrentine, Herbert C. "Johann Schobert and French Clavier Music from 1700 to the Revolution." 2 vols. Ph.D. diss., University of Iowa, 1962.

Tyson, Alan. "Clementi's Viennese Compositions 1781–82." *Music Review* 27 (1966): 16–24.

———. "The Date of Mozart's Piano Sonata in B-flat major, KV 333/315c: The 'Linz' Sonata?" In *Musik, Edition, Interpretation: Gedenkschrift Günter Henle*, edited by Martin Bente, 447–54. Munich: G. Henle Verlag, 1980.

———. Introduction. *Mozart: Piano Concerto No. 26 in D Major ("Coronation"), K. 537, The Autograph Score*. New York: Pierpont Morgan Library and Dover, 1991.

———. "The Mozart Fragments in the Mozarteum, Salzburg: A Preliminary Study of Their Chronology and Significance." *Journal of the American Musicological Society* 34 (Fall 1981): 471–510.

———. *Mozart, Studies of the Autograph Scores*. Cambridge: Harvard University Press, 1987.

———. "A Reconstruction of Nannerl Mozart's Music Book (Notenbuch)," *Music and Letters* 60 (1979): 389–400.

———. "Redating Mozart: Some Stylistic and Biographical Implications." Papers read at the forty-ninth annual meeting of the American Musicological Society. Louisville, Ky., 27–30 Oct. 1983.

Verchaly, André, ed. *Les influences étrangères dans l'oeuvre de W. A. Mozart*. Paris: Centre National de la Recherche Scientifique, 1958.

von Fischer, Kurt. "Das Dramatische in Mozarts Klavierkonzerten 1784 mit besonderer Berücksichtigung des ersten Satzes von KV 453." *MJb 1986*, 71–74.

———. "Mozarts Klaviervariationen: zur Editions- und Aufführungspraxis des späten 18. und frühen 19. Jahrhunderts." In *Hans Albrecht in Memoriam*, edited by Wilfried Brennecke and Hans Hasse, 168–73. Kassel: Bärenreiter, 1962.

———. Preface. *NMA*, Serie IX, *Klaviermusik*, Werkgruppe 26: *Variationen für Klavier*. Kassel: Bärenreiter, 1961.

Wainwright, David. *Broadwood, by Appointment*. London: Quiller Press, 1982.

Wolf, Eugene K. "On the Origins of the Mannheim Symphonic Style." In *Studies in Musicology in Honor of Otto E. Albrecht*, edited by John Walter Hill, 197–239. Kassel: Bärenreiter, 1980.

Wolff, Christoph. "New Research on Bach's *Musical Offering*". *Musical Quarterly* 57 (July 1971): 379–408.

———. Preface. *NMA*, Serie V, *Konzerte*, Werkgruppe 15: *Konzerte für ein oder mehrere Klaviere und Orchester mit Kadenzen*, Band 2. Kassel: Bärenreiter, 1976.

———. Preface. *NMA*, Serie V, *Konzerte*, Werkgruppe 15: *Konzerte für ein oder mehrere Klaviere und Orchester mit Kadenzen*, Band 3. Kassel: Bärenreiter, 1976.

———. "Über kompositionsgeschichtlichen Ort und Aufführungspraxis der Klavierkonzerte Mozarts." *MJb 1986*, 90–92.

———. "Zur Chronologie der Klavierkonzert-Kadenzen Mozarts." *MJb 1978–79*, 235–46.

Wyzewa, Théodore de, and Georges de Saint-Foix. *W.-A. Mozart, sa vie et son oeuvre de l'enfance a la pleine maturité*. 5 vols. Paris: Desclée de Brouwer et Cie, 1912–46.

Zaslaw, Neal. "The Classical Era: Introduction." In *Performance Practice, Music After 1600*, edited by Howard Mayer Brown and Stanley Sadie, 207–21. New York: Norton, 1989.

———. Jacket notes. John Eliot Gardiner, cond.; Malcolm Bilson, fortepiano; English Baroque Soloists. *Mozart: Concertos for Piano(s) and Orchestra (23); Rondo for Piano and Orchestra (2)*, Archiv Produktion CD: 427 317-2 (1989); 413 464-2 (1984); 413-463-2 (1984); 415 525-2 (1986); 427 846-2 (1987, 1988, 1989); 415 990-2 (1987); 410 905-2 (1984); 415 525-2 (1986).

———. "Leopold Mozart's List of His Son's Work." In *Music of the Classical Period: Essays in Honor of Barry S. Brook*, edited by Allan Atlas, 323–58. New York: Pendragon Press, 1985.

———. "Mozart's Paris Symphonies," *Musical Times* 119 (1978): 753–57.

———. *Mozart's Symphonies: Context, Performance Practice, Reception*. New York: Oxford University Press, 1989.

Zimmermann, Ewald. "Das Mozart-Preisausschreiben der Gesellschaft für Musikforschung." In *Festschrift Joseph Schmidt-Görg*, edited by Dagmar Weise, 400–408. Bonn: Beethovenhaus Verlag, 1957.

General Index

✳

Classified Index of Mozart's Keyboard Works

✳

Italic numbers designate pages on which music illustrations can be found.

Auernhammer sonatas, 45, 68, 69, 71, 125n.29. *See also* Chamber Music, Keyboard Works with Violin, K. 296, 376–380 (296, 374d, 374e, 317d, 373a, 374f)

Coronation Concerto, 106, 107. *See also* Concertos for Piano and Orchestra, K. 537

Dürnitz Sonata, 38, 45, 49, 50. *See also* Solo Works, Sonatas, K. 284 (205b)

J. C. Bach Concerto Arrangements, 7, 27, 80. *See also* Concerto Arrangements, K. 107/1–3 (21b)

Kegelstatt Trio, 89. *See also* Chamber Music, Piano Trios, K. 498

Palatinate Sonatas, 42, 45, 125n.29. *See also* Chamber Music, Keyboard Works with Violin, K. 301–306 (293a, 293b, 293c, 300c, 293d, 300l)

Pasticcio Concertos, 3, 7, 8, 80, 121n.8. *See also* Concerto Arrangements, K. 37, 39, 40, 41

SOLO WORKS

Sonatas

Sonata in G Major K. Anh. 199 (33d), lost, 33

Sonata in B-flat Major K. 200 (33e), lost, 33

Sonata in C Major K. 201 (33f), lost, 33

Sonata in F Major K. 202 (33g), lost, 33

Sonata in C Major K. 279 (189d), 32–37

Sonata in F Major K. 280 (189e), 32–37, *35*

Sonata in B-flat Major K. 281 (189f), 32–37, *36*

Sonata in E-flat Major K. 282 (189g), 32–37

Sonata in G Major K. 283 (189h), 32–37

Sonata in D Major K. 284 (205b), 32–35, 36–*37*, *38*, 45, 49–50

Sonata in C Major K. 309 (284b), 38, *39*, 40

Sonata in D Major K. 311 (284c), 38

Sonata in A Minor K. 310 (300d), 40, *41*, 42, *50*

Sonata in C Major K. 330 (300h), 46–47, 98, 125n.31

Sonata in A Major K. 331 (300i), 15, 46, 47, 98, 125n.31

Sonata in F Major K. 332 (300k), 46, 47–*48*, 98, 125n.31

Sonata in B-flat Major K. 333 (315c), 98–99

Sonata in C Minor K. 457, 13, 98, 99, 100–101

Sonata in F Major K. 533, 98, 101–*2*

Sonata in C Major K. 545, 98, 101

Sonata in F Major K. Anh. 135 (547a), 98

Sonata in B-flat Major K. 570, 98, 102–3

Sonata in D Major K. 576, 98, 102–3

Variations

Variations in G Major K. 24 on a Dutch Song, 9, 31

Variations in C Major K. 25 on Willem van Nassau, 9, 31

Variations in G Major K. 180 (173c) on "Mio caro Adone," 28, 31, 48, 49

Variations in C Major K. 179 (189a) on a minuet by J. C. Fischer, 28, 31–*32*, *33*, 48, 49

Variations in E-flat Major K. 354 (299a) on "Je Suis Lindor," 49

Variations in C Major K. 265 (300e) on "Ah vous dirai-je maman," 103

Variations in E-flat Major K. 353 (300f) on "La belle françoise," 103

Variations in C Major K. 264 (315d) on "Lison dormait," 49

Variations in F Major K. 352 (374c) on "Dieu d'amour," 103

Classified Index of Mozart's
Other Works

SONGS AND CANTATA

OPERAS, DRAMATIC WORK, AND ORATORIOS

SACRED WORKS